ARIZONA HIGHWAYS ALBUM

The Road To Statehood

1912

ARIZONA HIGHWAYS BOOK

C.W. Stevens' picnic wagon took Phoenix folks on desert outings in 1907.

Arizona Historical Society, Tucson

ARIZONA HIGHWAYS ALBUM

The Road to Statehood

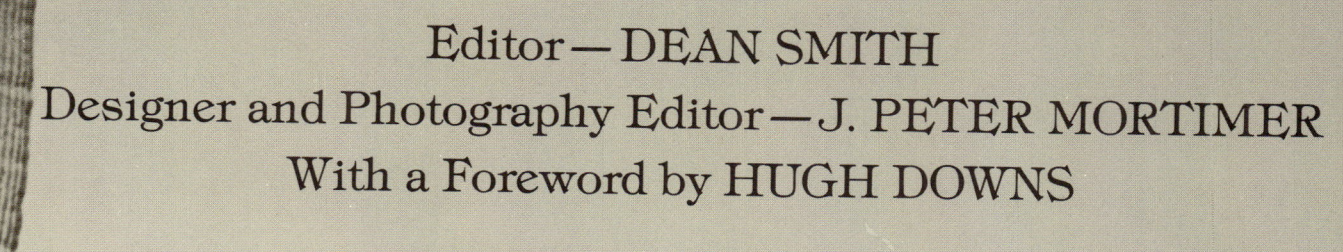

Editor — DEAN SMITH
Designer and Photography Editor — J. PETER MORTIMER
With a Foreword by HUGH DOWNS

Arizona Highways Album: The Road to Statehood was prepared
by the Related Products Section of *Arizona Highways* Magazine,
a monthly publication of the Arizona Department of Transportation.
Hugh Harelson, Publisher
Wesley Holden, Managing Editor, Related Products
Diana Pollock, Graphics and Production Manager

Contents

Foreword 8

Preface 9

CHAPTER I
Those Who Came Before 10
Striving for a Civilized Society 16
Bad Men and Law Men 32

CHAPTER II
Into a New Century 46
Arizona's Swing to Liberalism 56

CHAPTER III
The Longing for Statehood 76
Early Efforts for Statehood 82
Good Old Days? Bah, Humbug! 90

CHAPTER IV
Mr. Taft Says "No" 100
The Constitutional Convention of 1910 108
Theodore Roosevelt Dam 116

CHAPTER V

And the Bells Rang Out 124
Men Who Made the State 130
Now, B'Gosh, Even the Grub Tastes Better 138

CHAPTER VI

Launching a New State 148
State Government at Last 156
Incomparable George W.P. Hunt 164

CHAPTER VII

After Seventy-five Years 172
Arizona Today 174

Index 175

The continuing narrative in each chapter
was written by Dean Smith, Editor.

Copyright© 1987 by Arizona Department of Transportation, State of Arizona. All rights reserved. No part of this book may be reproduced in any form or by any means without permission from *Arizona Highways,* 2039 West Lewis Avenue, Phoenix, Arizona, 85009.

Library of Congress Catalog Number: 86-082099.

Arizona Highways Album 5

Acknowledgments

Like the pioneers of territorial days who put selfish interests aside to help a neighbor build a barn or recover lost livestock, Arizona's historical community enthusiastically answered the call of *Arizona Highways* to join forces in preparing this book celebrating the Diamond Jubilee of Arizona Statehood.

To say that *Arizona Highways Album: The Road to Statehood* has been a team effort would be grossly understating the case. Archivists from historical museums and libraries throughout the state — twenty-three of them — searched their files for photographs depicting life in Arizona during the battle for statehood. The National Archives and the Library of Congress made their resources available, as did museums in California. Several private collections loaned priceless photographs. Before the search was ended, editors examined well over 5,000 images, from which 235 were chosen for publication in this book.

Among the contributing writers are some of Arizona's most respected historians and widely-read story tellers. Like the photo archivists and librarians, they combined their talents to bring to life an exciting period of Arizona history. To all these knowledgeable people, and to those whose expertise put the images and words together in so artistic a manner, we are grateful.

Hugh Harelson
Publisher
Arizona Highways

The editors are grateful to the following photography repositories for their cooperation: Arizona Highways Magazine • Arizona Historical Foundation • Arizona Historical Society, Flagstaff • Arizona Historical Society, Phoenix • Arizona Historical Society, Tucson • Arizona Historical Society, Yuma • Arizona State University Archives • Arizona State University Library • Bancroft Library, University of California • Benson Historical Society • Bisbee Mining and Historical Museum • Center for Creative Photography, University of Arizona • Cochise County Historical Society, Douglas • Robert Creighton Collection • Department of Library, Archives and Public Records, State of Arizona • Desert Caballeros Western Museum, Wickenburg • Indiana State Historical Society • Eileen Joyce Collection • Library of Congress • Herb and Dorothy McLaughlin Collection • Mesa Southwest Museum • Leonard Monti Collection • National Archives • Northern Arizona University Library • Salt River Project • Sharlot Hall Museum, Prescott • Tempe Historical Museum • University of Arizona Library

The following Arizona companies were involved in this book's production: W. A. Krueger (printing) • Ingram Paper • Roswell Bookbinding • Royal Custom House (photography preparation) • ProType (typography) • Cover Design by Wayne Baker

map of ARIZONA 1912

drawn by Don Bufkin

Scale in Miles: 0, 25, 50

County Boundaries
Railroads ┼┼┼
○ Unincorporated Mining Towns

Incorporated Towns by Population Size based upon 1910 Census data

- **TUCSON** ⊙ over 10,000
- **Bisbee** ● 2,000 to 10,000
- **Mesa** ● 1,000 to 1,999

Counties
MOHAVE, COCONINO, NAVAJO, APACHE, YAVAPAI, YUMA, MARICOPA, GILA, GREENLEE, PINAL, GRAHAM, PIMA, COCHISE, SANTA CRUZ

Indian Reservations
KAIBAB IND. RES., HAVASUPAI IND. RES., HUALAPAI IND. RES., NAVAJO IND. RES., HOPI IND. RES., COLORADO RIVER IND. RES., FORT APACHE IND. RES., SAN CARLOS IND. RES., GILA RIVER IND. RES., PAPAGO IND. RES., SAN XAVIER IND. RES.

Towns
Chloride, Oatman & Goldroad, Kingman, Williams, Grand Canyon, Flagstaff, Winslow, Prescott, Jerome, Congress, Swansea, Crown King, Kofa & Polaris, Glendale, PHOENIX, Tempe, Mesa, Roosevelt Dam, Globe, Miami, Ray, Morenci, Clifton, Florence, Hayden, Yuma, Silverbell, Twin Buttes, TUCSON, Pearce, Courtland & Gleeson, Tombstone, Bisbee, Nogales, Douglas

Rivers
Colorado River, Little Colorado River, Verde River, Gila River, San Pedro River, Santa Cruz River

Railroads
A.T. & S.F.R.R., S.P.R.R.

Arizona Highways Album 7

Foreword

By Hugh Downs

It is nineteen years now since my wife and I decided to make Arizona our home. I've written often about how we came to choose this state, after realizing we had both lost our Midwest roots, and how we persuaded my father to come from Ohio to join us in what turned out to be the last (and, according to his sworn statement, most enjoyable) decade of his life; and of all the chamber of commerce claims about climate and congeniality which are easily true; and of the dimension *beyond* satisfaction that has long since justified our decision.

But from this vantage point a feeling has been distilled that now haunts me with understanding: understanding what Joseph Wood Krutch felt about the Sonoran Desert, when, after a career as a New York journalist, he was involved in the establishment of Tucson's Desert Museum and knew for the rest of his life he was home. Understanding the feelings of historian Bert Fireman when he spoke to me of the Hohokam and the engineering achievements of the "People Who Came Before," and the time-depth that outdistanced the tribal memory of Native Americans living among us now.

The practical, vital, solid life I enjoy as an Arizona resident is now complemented by an underlying pedal-tone I had not heard when we first moved out to Carefree: history and prehistory are not discontinuous. The petroglyph in the almost inaccessible place, the unvisited pueblos in a cliff cave on the San Carlos Indian Reservation, the remains of ancient irrigation canals — are from the same impetus as Phoenix's Sky Harbor Airport expansion or the Hilton and Hyatt Regency hotels. Nor is the variety of terrain discontinuous. The tall grass and piñon pine and ponderosa above the Mogollon Rim are one with the saguaro and ocotillo and strawberry hedgehog and prickly pear to the south. There is enormous variety within a unity that is Arizona.

My heirs would be dismayed to know how much I would give to be able to spend one hour in Yuma during the steamboat days, or to have been with Garcia Lopez de Cardenas when his party first saw the Grand Canyon. Or to have seen downtown Phoenix when Jim Hardy (who was ninety-six when I met him in 1970) ran away from home at age thirteen. (He ran across a formidable nine-mile stretch of desert between Phoenix and Glendale!)

But I settle for getting on a horse and striking off into the Mazatzal Wilderness for two or three days. Or just looking from my house to South Mountain. At different times of day, this view forms thousands of pictures.

It is still the Arizona Territory. Happily, it also is a state, and this year we celebrate the seventy-fifth anniversary of statehood. But that condition has simply been added to it and takes nothing away from the grandeur of being a zone of the continent that is like nothing else anywhere in the world.

I'm glad I wasn't born in Arizona. I might have taken it for granted. To come to it after living in many other places lets me know its worth in a way difficult for the native. Like a religious convert, I feel I have an added point of pride in having *chosen* it.

Preface

North of the community of Cave Creek there are traces of a road into the mountains, built for stagecoaches running up to Prescott, and stone ruins we local people believe to be what's left of a station. Every time I ride past this forlorn pile of rocks overgrown now with ironwood and mesquite, I have a vision of myself standing near the doorway, someone else leading horses away from the stage, dust rising from the area in front of the corral. (There is not much dust now because of the choking vegetation.) I have large moustaches in this vision; I'm wearing a dark vest and a heavy Colt Dragoon revolver hangs at my side. Why do I imagine this to be myself? Who have I been? I do not have such visions in other places, other states or countries.

If such a strong feeling — romantic and swashbuckling and cliché — is not evidence I should be put under close surveillance, then it is indication I belong in Arizona.

Perhaps sometime in the far future, someone will hover over the ruins of Interstate 17 — all conveyances, public and private, will then move above the ground — and have a vision of me on my way to Lake Pleasant. And he will wonder why he sees me as himself. But he will know he belongs in Arizona.

HUGH DOWNS is one of the most familiar figures in the history of American television. Currently the host of ABC-TV News' 20/20 show, he has won acclaim as a news reporter, interviewer, host, and narrator. For nearly two decades he has made his home at Carefree, Arizona, north of Scottsdale. He has grown to love Arizona with a passion equaled by few lifelong residents of the state.

The people of Arizona have not been celebrating Statehood Day anniversaries for very long. Indeed, many who took part in the memorable events of that Valentine's Day, February 14, 1912, are still prominent in the affairs of Arizona. Senator Barry Goldwater served that day as ring bearer at the first wedding conducted in the new state. Flagstaff's remarkable Viola Passey Babbitt, civic leader *par excellence,* was a Tempe Normal schoolgirl on that date. Many other noted Arizona oldsters have watched all seventy-five years of statehood from ringside seats.

Yet the time will come, and too soon, when we can remember the exciting events leading up to Statehood Day only from the written record, and from the images made by the simple cameras of the day. Then we can only wonder how it was — and how *we* were — in that boisterous, optimistic era when all things seemed possible, and people could scarcely wait a day to start building one of the truly great states of the American Union.

Arizona Highways Album: The Road to Statehood focuses on how Arizona lived, worked, played, loved, and dreamed in the decade leading up to statehood, and in our early years as the Baby State.

We have acknowledged our debt to the past centuries in the opening chapter and noted the achievements of the past seventy-five years in the final one, but this book is primarily a chronicle of Arizona's passage into statehood. We hope all Arizonans, natives and newcomers, will find the story a fascinating one.

Chapter I
Those Who Came Before

Arizona was not discovered first by the Moor Esteban, Fray Marcos de Niza, or Coronado in 1539-40. These Europeans were late arrivals who chanced upon a Native American civilization that had been thriving in relative peace and prosperity for many centuries. The Hopi village of Old Oraibi (below) in northern Arizona has been continuously inhabited since A.D. 1100, some five hundred years before the first English colonists arrived at Jamestown, Virginia. Arizona's earliest settlers built cliff dwellings and stone villages, developed agriculture and crafts, and worshipped their gods while Europe was still emerging from the Dark Ages.

Arizona Historical Society, Tucson

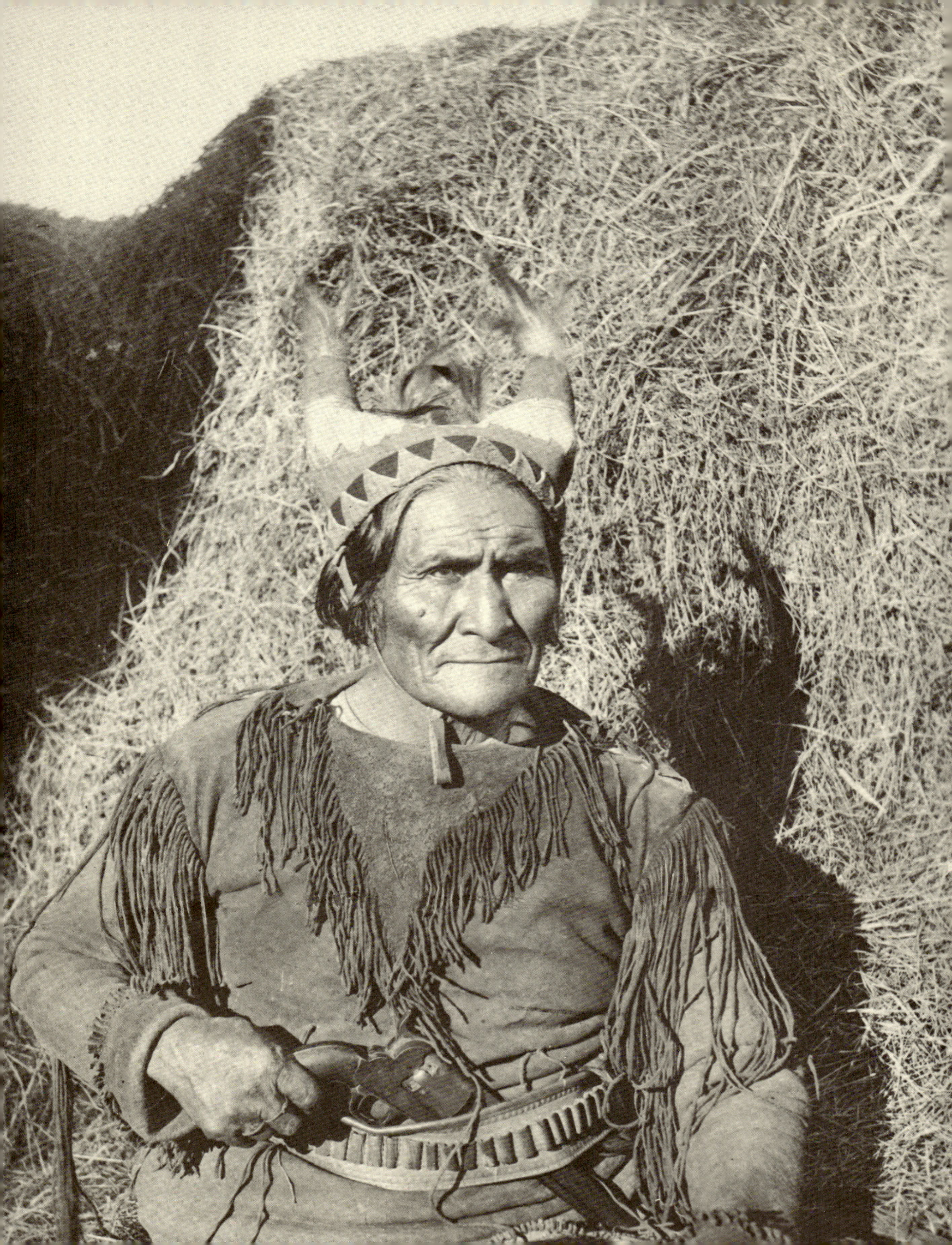

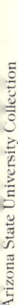

Geronimo (left), whose fame surpassed that of several other great leaders of the Chiricahua Apaches, harassed white interlopers for more than two decades before his surrender in 1886. Like the fabled Cochise before him, Geronimo used stealth and mobility to strike telling blows and then vanish into the mountains of southeastern Arizona and northern Mexico.

Much of Arizona's early history is a story of whites warring against Indian tribes, and eventual pacification or resettlement of the native peoples, whose cultures have been preserved. The Hopi ceremonials on the arid mesas of northeastern Arizona still include the snake dancer (above). The Havasupai gentleman (above right) lived with his family in 1901 in a portion of the Grand Canyon. The young Apache mother and her baby (right) lived at that same time near the present site of Roosevelt Dam.

Arizona Highways Album 13

Father Eusebio Kino founded the mission called San Xavier del Bac in 1700. The beautiful structure south of Tucson, known today as the "White Dove of the Desert," was started in 1783 and was fourteen years in the building.

Amazing Arizona, land of startling contrasts, is a new state in a setting that once nurtured ancient cave dwellers and the mammoths they hunted for sustenance.

Primitive man battled the forces of nature here more than 50,000 years ago. Yet the principal body of Arizona's written history is little more than a century old. If we may impose those 50,000 years on a twenty-four-hour clock, Arizona's emergence as a frontier territory did not occur until two minutes before midnight.

It was not until the Civil War era that Arizona had a permanent population large enough to warrant separate territorial status. The first official census in 1864 revealed that only 4,573 residents (untamed Indians were not counted) lived in the newly-created Arizona Territory.

We have abundant evidence that the hardy ancients migrated from Asia to Alaska and then southward to what is now Arizona. Native Americans farmed and built irrigation systems and created beautiful works of art all over Arizona for many centuries before the arrival of the Spanish conquistadores changed their way of life for all time to come.

Francisco Vasquez de Coronado made the first extensive exploration of Arizona and the American Southwest — all the way to Kansas — in 1540-41. Later visits by Antonio de Espejo (1583) and Juan de Oñate (1598) added to the world's knowledge of this mysterious land.

At the end of the seventeenth century, such heroic priests as Father Eusebio Francisco Kino made their way across northern Mexico to what was then known as the Pimeria Alta — Sonora and Arizona. They came to Christianize the Indians, extend Spanish civilization, and build such magically beautiful

Continued on page 40

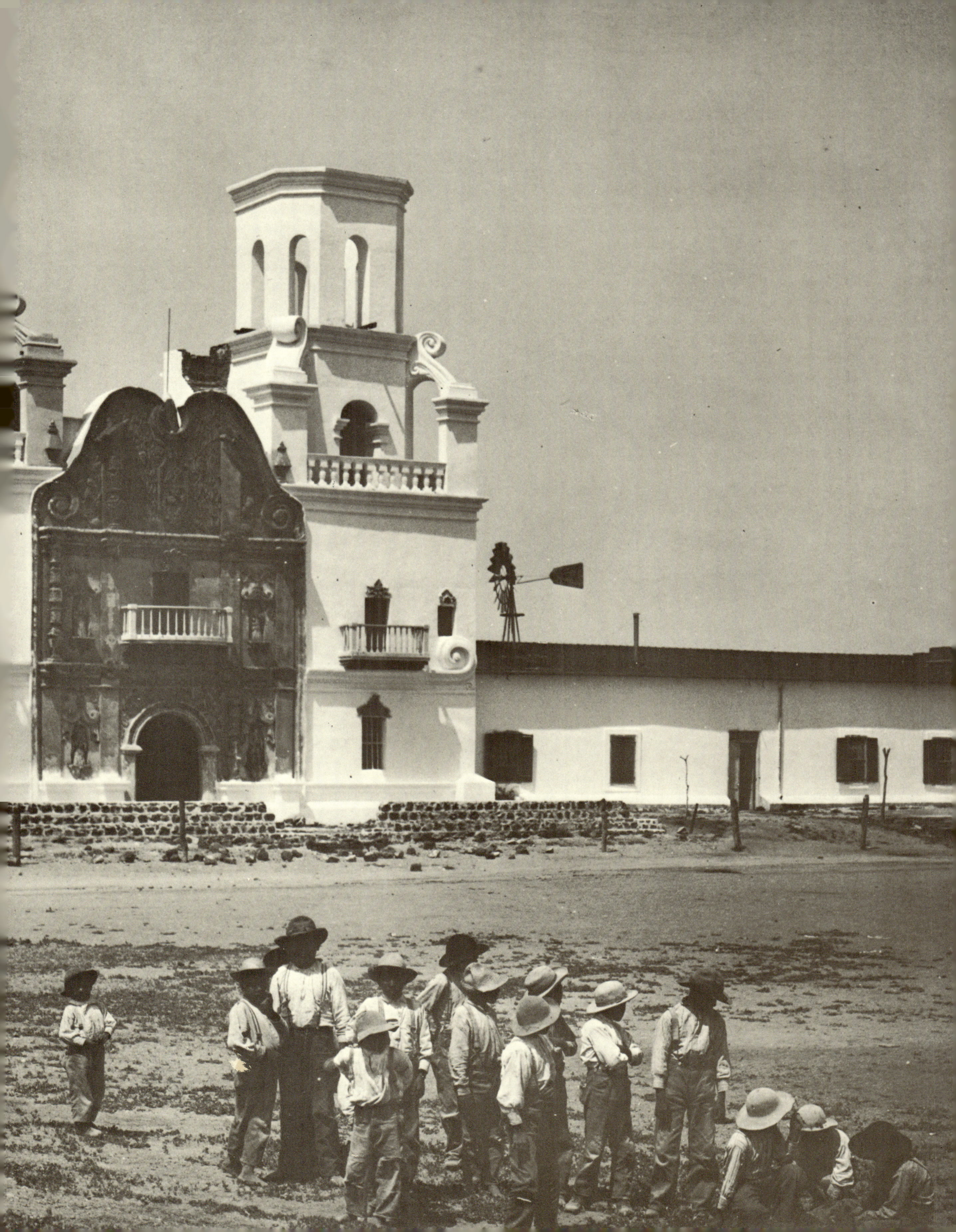

Striving for a Civilized Society

By Robert A. Trennert

Senator Benjamin Wade once said that Arizona was just like Hell: all it needed was water and good society. Although this sarcastic remark might have been appropriate at the time Arizona became a separate territory in 1863, by the last two decades of the nineteenth century everything had changed, and Arizonans considered themselves ready for admission to the Union. Indeed, the eighties and nineties saw the territory cast off much of its frontier lifestyle, becoming in the process a more settled, stable, progressive, and, yes, civilized place.

These changes came about because the territory managed to resolve a number of problems that had combined to limit growth and economic development. One of the biggest drawbacks was Indian hostilities, in particular those involving the Apaches. But with the final surrender of Geronimo in 1886, the Indian wars came to a conclusion, and the native population was confined to reservations. Although many Arizonans hoped to have the Indians removed to Oklahoma, the establishment of reservations made possible a period of economic growth.

Enhancing this situation even more was the coming of the railroads, which allowed Arizonans to exploit the resources of the territory. Railroad construction came relatively late, but, once begun, it spread rapidly. The Southern Pacific entered the territory at Yuma in 1879, reached Tucson the following year, and quickly extended to El Paso, putting southern Arizona on the transcontinental main line. Soon thereafter, the Atlantic and Pacific (later Santa Fe) laid its line across northern Arizona. The completion of these railroads opened the territory.

Immediately, branch lines were constructed in every direction, and, by the turn of the century, nearly every major mining and commercial center had rail connections. Supplies and manufactured goods from the outside could not be obtained at reasonable prices, and the products of Arizona found a market.

Arizona had three economic legs — mining, ranching, and farming — which produced enough prosperity to bring the territory into the modern world at the end of the century. Mineral wealth, in particular, became important during these years. Gold and silver

Continued on page 22

When President Lincoln created the Arizona Territory on February 24, 1863, he appointed territorial officers who barely knew where Arizona was on the map. Their first goal in the wild new land was to survive, and only later could they give thought to bringing the amenities of civilization to the territory. Shortly after they arrived and set up a temporary seat of government at Camp Whipple in Chino Valley, they posed for a photograph (above). John Goodwin, first governor to serve in Arizona, is seated second from right. Richard McCormick, who succeeded Goodwin as governor, is seated at far right. Frontier dress was functional, but carefully chosen, as demonstrated by this cowgirl (right) of a slightly later period. But the pioneers put on the trappings of eastern civilization as soon as conditions permitted.

16   Arizona Highways Album

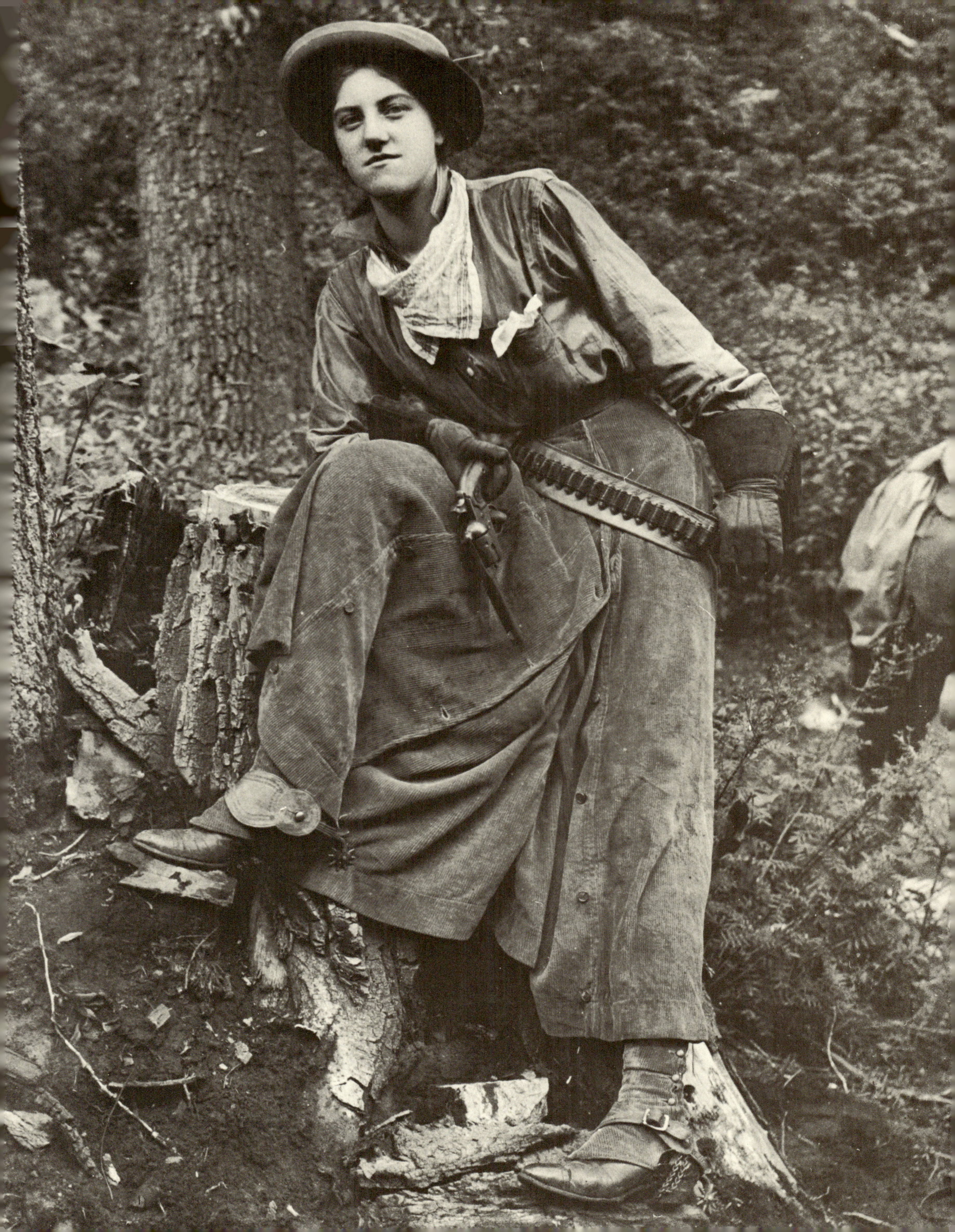

Arizona Highways Album

Tempe Historical Museum

Leonard Monti Collection

The arrival of the Atlantic and Pacific Railroad (now Santa Fe) in Flagstaff in 1882 opened a great new era of prosperity in northern Arizona. Now the Arizona Lumber and Timber Company, operated by transplanted Chicagoans Mike and Tim Riordan, could ship its products from Flagstaff to eastern markets (left). The Babbitt Brothers, who came to Flagstaff from Cincinnati in 1886, could transport their cattle and bring in merchandise for their stores. Everybody benefited.

Train robberies were relatively rare, but highly publicized. Most costly were the bridge washouts, train derailments, and wrecks. Some were spectacular, such as this late 1890s catastrophe on the bridge at Tempe (above).

(Following pages) Gambling was a legal and very popular activity in Arizona Territory until just before the achieving of statehood. Gamblers were regularly elected to public office; Prescott's W.O. (Buckey) O'Neill of Spanish-American War fame earned his nickname at the faro table; and gamblers provided the land in Tucson for the University of Arizona campus. Often, gambling was a genteel and scientific endeavor, as in this faro game at the famed Orient Saloon in Bisbee, photographed by W.E. Irwin. Stakes were high at Arizona gaming tables, and cheaters sometimes paid with their lives.

Bisbee Mining and Historical Museum

Arizona Historical Society, Flagstaff

Arizona Highways Album 19

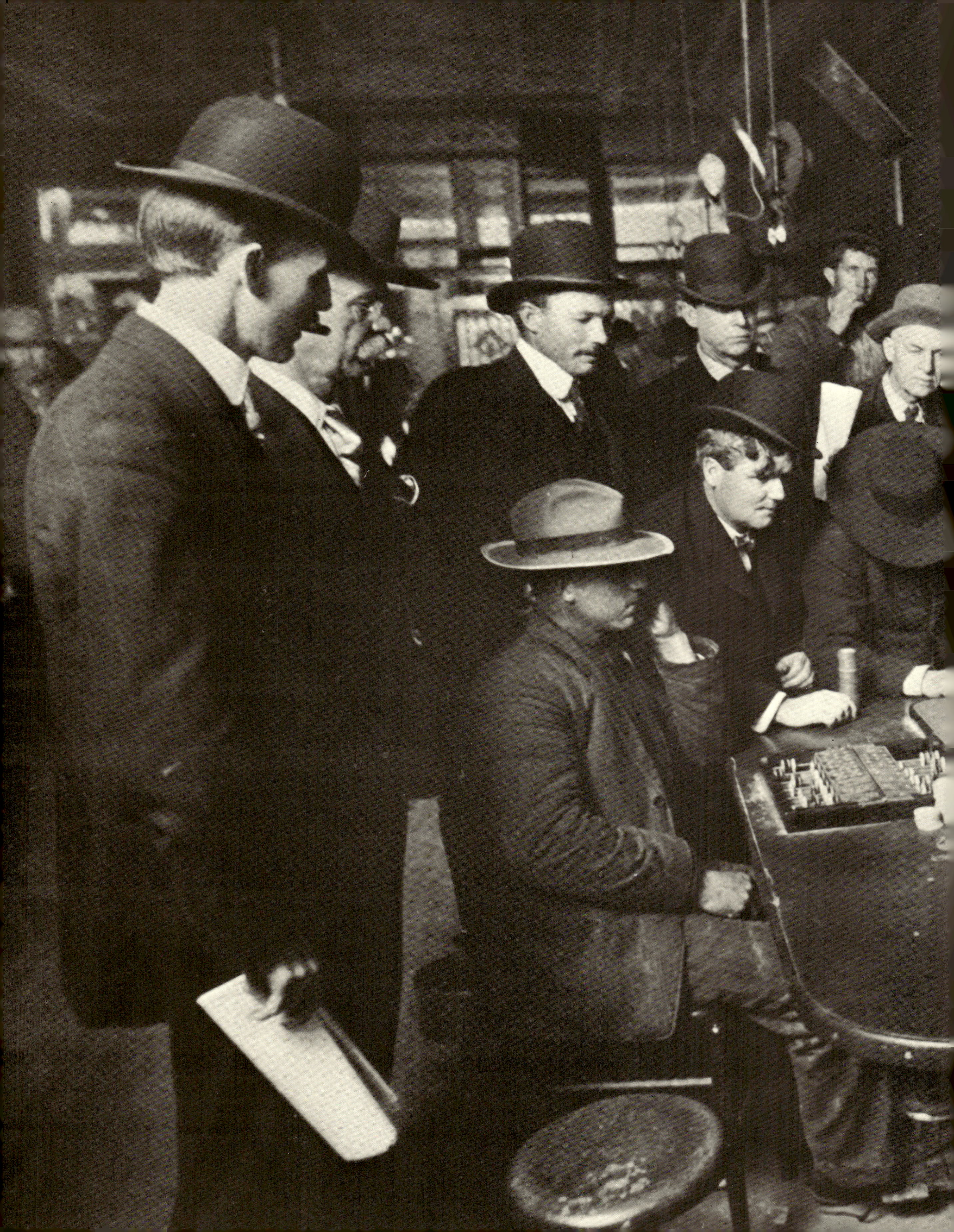

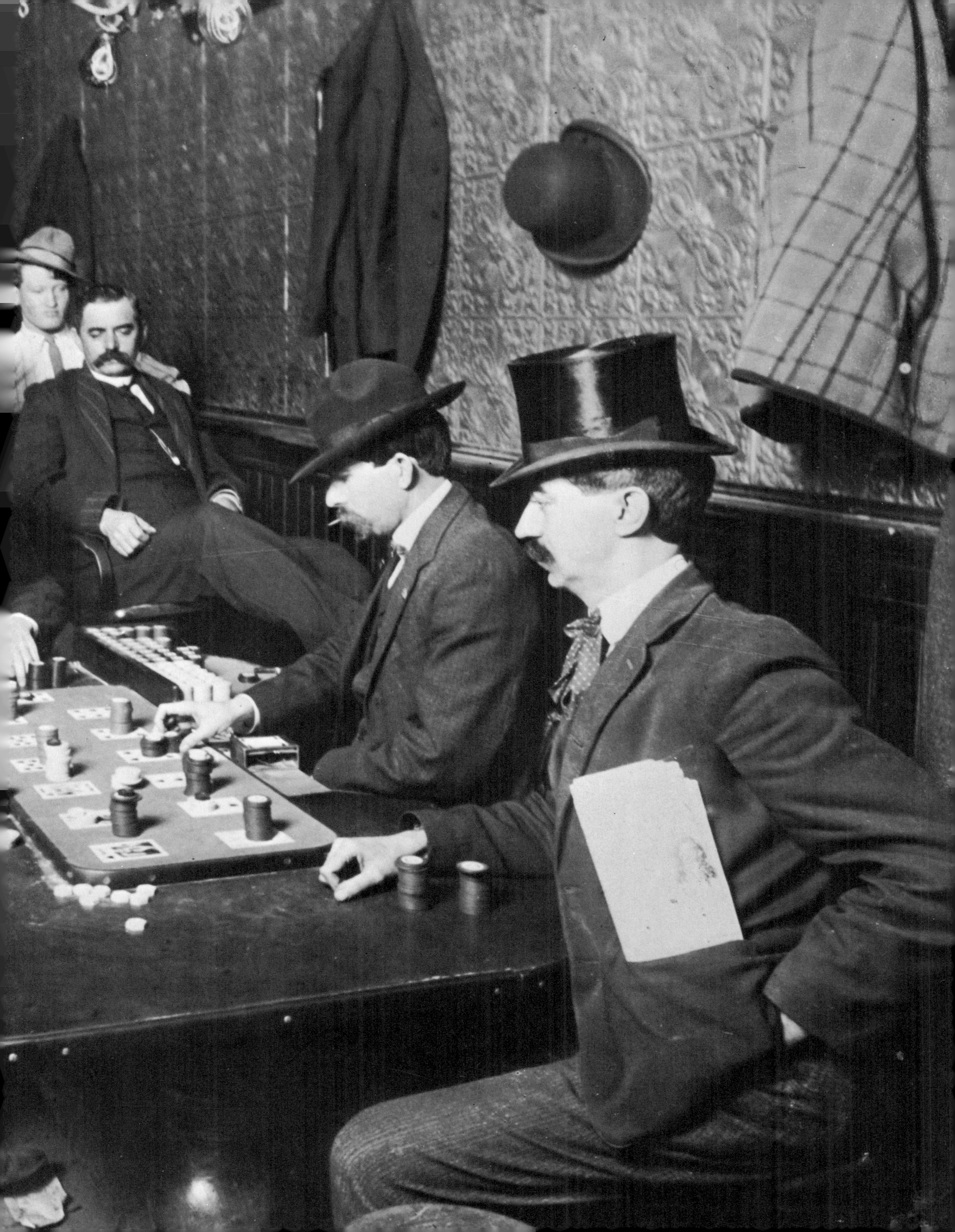

Arizona Historical Society, Yuma

Continued from page 16

mining, which had been restricted by Apache warriors and a lack of transportation, produced significant bonanzas between 1865 and 1885. Mining districts near Prescott and Wickenburg and camps such as Tombstone became major producers, filling those regions with miners, merchants, speculators, saloonkeepers, and prostitutes.

Even more significant, copper production replaced gold and silver in economic importance during the 1880s. By the end of the decade, Arizona's copper mines were more valuable than any other resource. More than half a dozen copper districts blossomed during this period, bringing into existence such rip-roaring communities as Clifton-Morenci, Bisbee, Globe, Ray, and Jerome. The names of Longfellow, Copper Queen, and United Verde mines became household words as Arizonans enjoyed the reward of their hard work and perseverance.

Ranching, too, contributed to the prosperity. Cattle had been in the Santa Cruz Valley since the 1700s, but, during the 1880s, open range grazing dominated Arizona. Thousands of cattle roamed rangelands from the Sulphur Springs Valley to the northern plateau. Hispanic, Black, and Anglo cowboys, in all their rustic glory, worked on ranches with such exotic names as Hashknife, Chiricahua, and Empire, while cattle barons Henry Hooker, Pete Kitchen, and others held sway in Arizona's social and political circles.

During the 1890s, ranching suffered a setback as prices plummeted, forcing the range bosses to modernize. The use of barbed wire allowed fencing of the range, while windmills and veterinary science enabled ranchers to improve their herds. At the turn of the century, the cattle industry had seen its glory day, but it had also matured, contributing greatly to the economic stability of Arizona Territory.

More important for the future was the beginning of large-scale agriculture. Water proved the key as farming regions such as the Salt River Valley grew rapidly. Prehistoric Indian canals were re-excavated, creating a vast agricultural region that would grow almost anything. As it entered the present century, Arizona was raising vast crops of citrus, alfalfa, vegetables, and fruit, all of which fostered a farm boom unlike anything the Southwest had seen.

All of these factors contributed to the economic maturity of Arizona. They also convinced residents that they were ready for statehood. Adding to this passionate feeling was a change in the political tradition, spurred in part by the increasing trend toward urbanization. Arizona's towns developed in impressive fashion. As they did, they demanded the cultural amenities that eastern critics accused them of lacking.

Phoenix proved to be a prime example. Not settled until 1867, by the eighties the city was emerging as Arizona's major metropolis. City fathers, backed by a group of enthusiastic boosters, engineered a number of moves designed to place Phoenix on the map and enhance its business prospects. In rapid order, the Territorial Asylum was opened in 1886; railroad connections arrived in 1887; and the federal Indian school was constructed in 1891. In 1889 local boosters managed their greatest coup by securing the territorial capital.

These events enhanced urban growth and development considerably. Urban Phoenicians, of course, did not want to be left out of Victorian cultural trends; so they joined fraternal, charitable, and religious organizations, built opera houses and theaters, and indulged themselves as much as possible in intellectual and cultural stimulation. When these activities were combined with similar developments in Tucson, Prescott, and Bisbee and the opening of the University of Arizona, the territory

Continued on page 29

From the day in 1852 when the Uncle Sam made its first trip up the Colorado River, steamboating on the historic waterway played a vital role in civilizing and supplying Arizona Territory. Until the railroads were built in the 1880s, steamboats offered the best and cheapest means of bringing passengers and freight from California ports to Yuma and Ehrenberg. Searchlight, Gila, and other popular craft plied the river for more than four decades.

Although they were essentially cargo ships, the steamboats provided modest comforts for passengers. Fares from San Francisco to Yuma were in the forty to eighty dollar range in the 1870s.

(Left) Yumans of the early days had less than palatial housing. These huts of mud and poles were still in use after the railroad came. (Right) Dressed in Victorian finery, two ladies and a child wait patiently on the top deck for the arrival of their steamer, St. Valier, in 1894. (Below) Heavy Colorado River steamboat traffic at Yuma necessitated construction of an elaborate swing bridge, shown opening to allow a sternwheeler to pass.

Arizona Historical Society, Yuma

Arizona Historical Society, Yuma

Arizona Highways Album

Arizona Historical Society, Tucson

Arizona State University Library

Arizona Historical Society, Tucson

Arizona State University Library

Arizona Territory citizens lived most of their lives in the out-of-doors. Whether at work or play, Arizonans of those decades before air conditioning usually were to be found under the open sky. (Top left) Cowboys like this one on a Santa Cruz County ranch detested any work that couldn't be done from the saddle of a horse. (Top center) Deer hunting in the Chiricahua Mountains of Cochise County was a popular sport, as was lion hunting (above) along the Mexican border. (Top right) Farmers in northern Arizona were glad they had big families when it came time to cut the hay. (Right) Ready for a day in the saddle, these cowboys at the Q Ranch in Pleasant Valley gather by the ranch house.

24   Arizona Highways Album

Arizona Historical Society, Tucson

Bisbee Mining and Historical Museum

McLaughlin Collection

Arizona State University Library

Bisbee Mining and Historical Museum

Mining was Arizona's earliest economic mainstay, and it continued to be so until well after statehood. First gold and then copper provided the wealth to build a prosperous territory.

(Upper left) The grim faces of these Bisbee copper miners reveal how exhausting and dispiriting was early-day labor in Arizona's mines. (Center left) Loading supplies for the mines on mule trains, these teamsters line up along Jefferson Street in Phoenix. (Lower left) Wood — mountains of it — was needed for tunnel supports, charcoal-making, and other uses at the Silver King Mine east of the Superstition Mountains. (Above) The great smelters, such as this one at Bisbee in 1898, turned ore into gleaming copper. (Right) The creekside fortune hunter with his gold panning equipment was the first to arrive in Arizona. This old-timer tries his luck in the Colorado River.

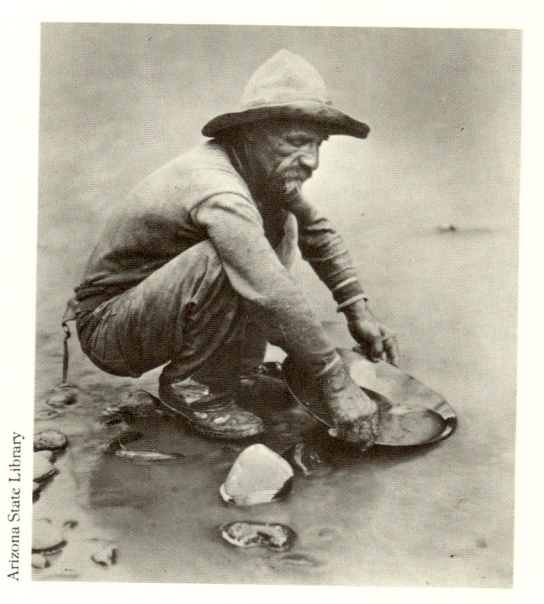

Arizona State Library

Arizona Highways Album 27

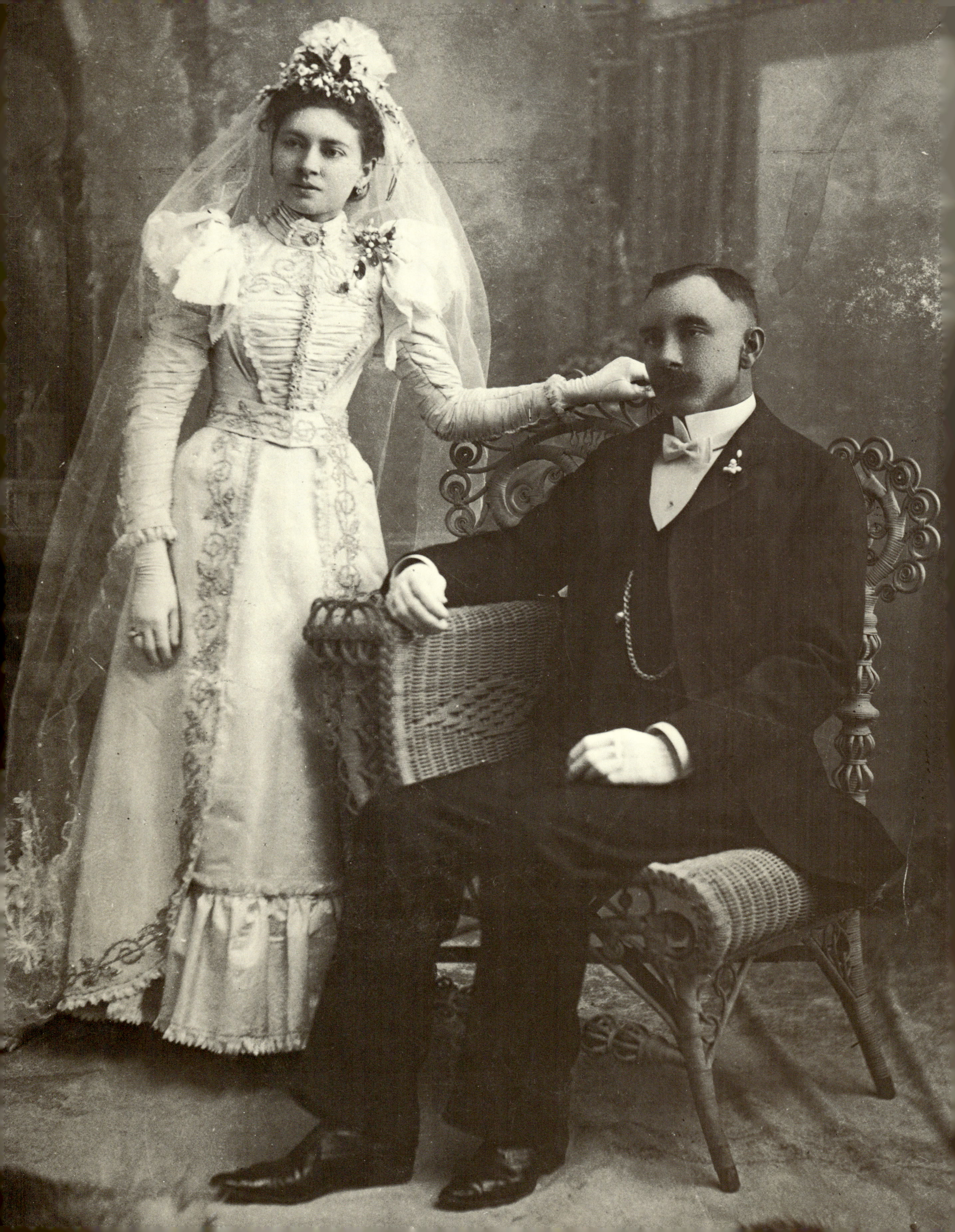

Arizonans were conscious of their "Wild West" image, so they sometimes went to great lengths to put on the trappings of civilization. (Left) Carmen Celaya and Demetrio Amado were spectacularly attired for their formal wedding in Tucson. (Below) Gaiety reigned supreme at this young people's party in Phoenix in 1892. Dress was a bit more formal than at today's social gatherings.

McLaughlin Collection

Continued from page 22

made great strides in proving that it was no longer a lawless and wild frontier.

In a political sense, the last two decades of the century have been classified by one historian as the "Cosmopolitan Era." Arizonans ended their dependence on federally appointed officials, preferring instead to support a group of politicians who made their homes in Arizona and advocated local issues. Leading this group were Governor Nathan O. Murphy and Congressional Delegate Marcus A. Smith, both of whom rose to prominence in the eighties and nineties.

Their most popular activity was supporting statehood. Smith, Murphy, and other Arizonans argued that the territory had matured enough to earn a place in the Union. During the 1890s, they organized conventions, petitioned Congress, and took straw votes. They also flooded Congress with propaganda showing that Arizona possessed the required population, economic strength, and cultural refinement to be considered equal.

Unfortunately, no one in Congress listened. To that body, Arizona remained a sparsely populated, forbidding area. Arizona had indeed become civilized, but the rest of the country was unconvinced. So statehood was delayed.

ROBERT A. TRENNERT, chair of the Department of History at Arizona State University, has earned a national reputation for his scholarship, teaching, and efforts in historical preservation. Frontier and Indian history are his specialities. His writings include Alternative to Extinction *and* Indian Traders of the Middle Border.

Arizona Highways Album 29

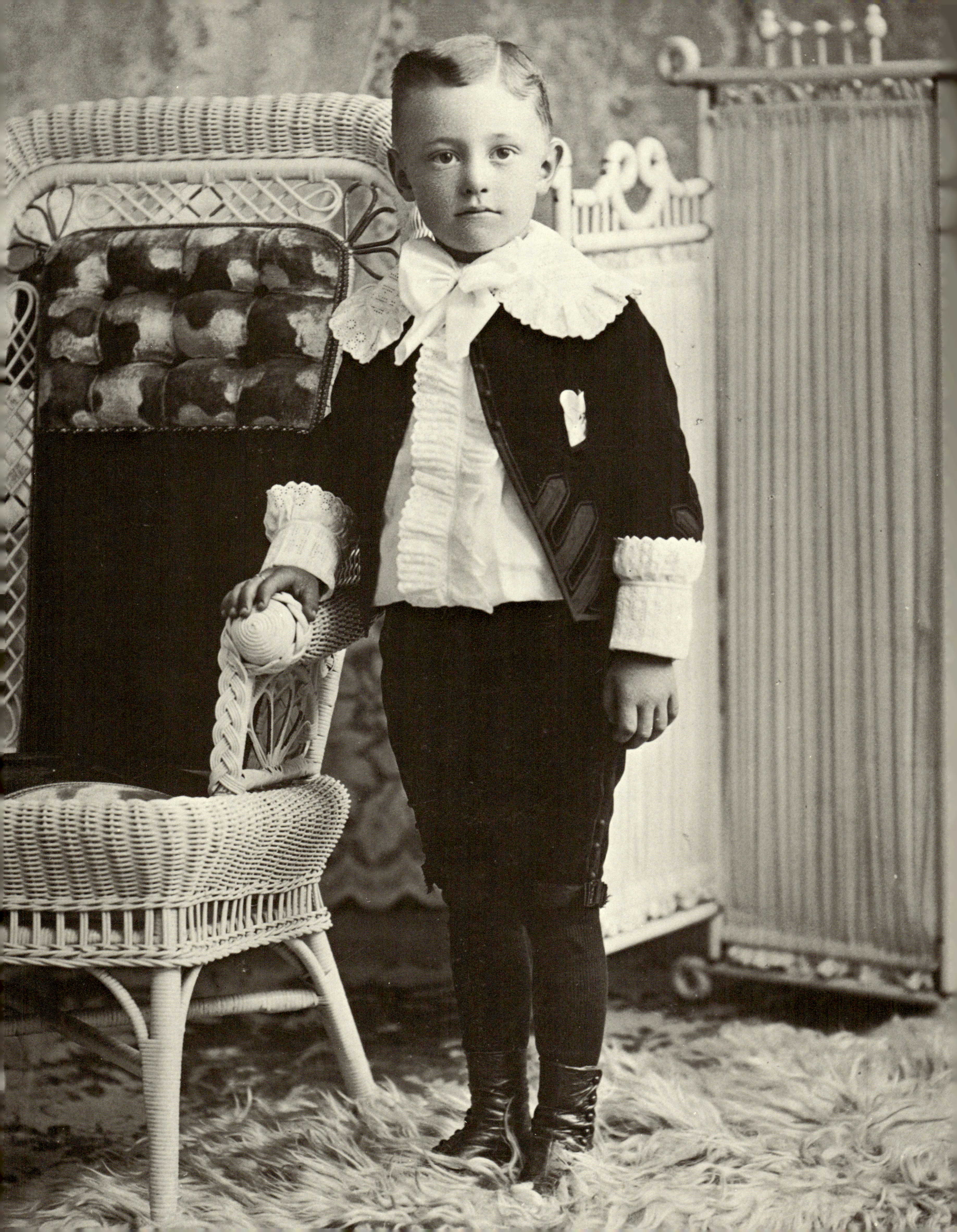

Arizonans dressed their children in their Sunday best for a visit to the portrait photographer. (Left) Young Garland Ross of Prescott was Little Lord Fauntleroy himself in his collar and ruffles. (Below) Euretta Penuimburg, also of Prescott, was preparing for a career as a tea hostess.

Sharlot Hall Museum

Bad Men and Law Men

By Marshall Trimble

Entire libraries may be stocked with the dime novels, paperbacks and western adventure stories involving Arizona outlaws and the men who devoted their lives to putting those outlaws behind bars or on the gallows. It seems certain that Arizona's lurid reputation as a haven for the lawless element delayed the achieving of statehood.

(Right) Inmates at the Arizona Territorial Prison in Yuma in the mid-1890s paid dearly for their crimes. It was one of the toughest—and hottest—prisons in the West. Their broad-brimmed hats helped shield them from the merciless sun. (Below) These Tucson lawmen carried enough arms and ammunition to fight a small war, and they needed every bit of it.

Arizona's reputation as the West's last refuge for hard-bitten desperados was a major reason its admittance to statehood was delayed so long.

The proximity to the Mexican border, bad roads, poor communication, and rugged terrain made pursuit and capture of outlaws almost impossible. To make matters worse, rural residents were sometimes hesitant to assist peace officers because many of their neighbors were outlaws, and they didn't want to incur vengeance.

The hard men who rode the Arizona Territory were products of a lawless and violent post-Civil War era characterized by range wars, feuds, Apache fighting, and the lust for gold and silver. Today they and their deeds have slipped from reality into the realm of romance. Trail dust has settled and the false-front saloons are gone, but their stories linger on and are deeply ingrained in our culture.

The types of men hired to keep the peace were as varied as the rest of the wide gamut of frontier society. Jeff Milton was the son of a Florida governor; Wyatt Earp was a restless entrepreneur whose skill with a six-shooter and nerves of steel made him a formidable adversary; Jim Roberts earned his reputation as a fearless gunfighter

Arizona Historical Society, Yuma

Arizona Historical Society, Tucson

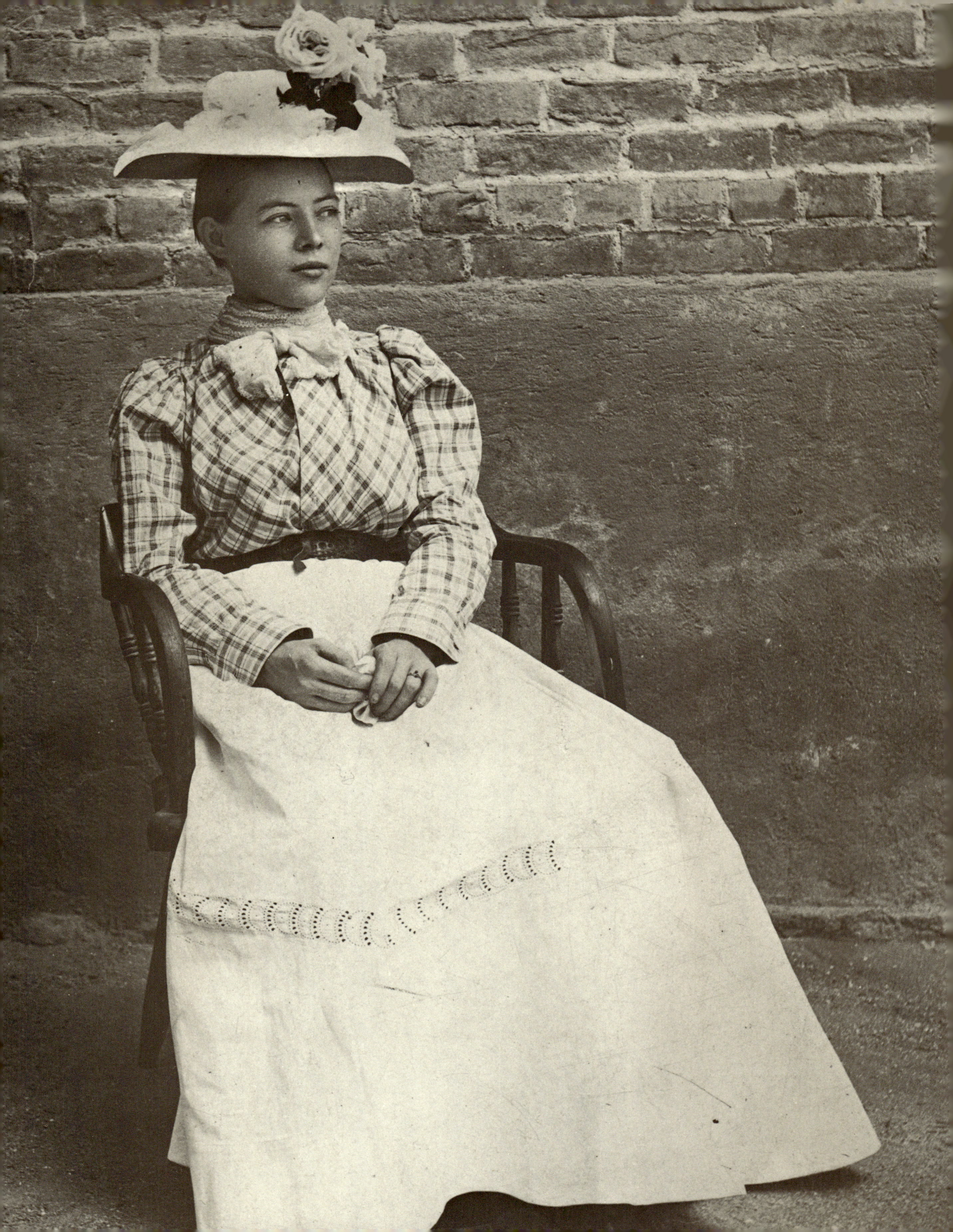

during the Pleasant Valley War; Burt Mossman was a rawhide-tough ranch boss before he was appointed first captain of the Arizona Rangers; and Carl Hayden was a Stanford graduate with political hopes.

All had one thing in common: they had little fear of God and none of the ole Devil.

Milton is best known for his part in breaking up the Fairbank train robbery in February, 1900. Bravo Juan Yoas, Three-finger Jack Dunlap, and three cronies decided to rob the Wells Fargo express car while the train was stopped at Fairbank. However, the outlaws didn't figure on Jeff Milton riding shotgun in the express car.

They opened fire as the train pulled in, and a bullet struck the lawman as he stood in the open door of the car. Bleeding from a wound in his arm, Milton opened up with a 10-gauge sawed-off scattergun. Three-finger took a full, fatal blast while Bravo Juan took evasive action and caught a load of buckshot in the seat of the pants. They didn't get the strongbox and were eventually captured. Milton survived and died with his boots off in Tucson in 1947.

Earp made his reputation during the so-called "Gunfight at the OK Corral," or Cochise County War, in the early 1880s. Wyatt and his brothers Morgan and Virgil, along with their pal Doc Holliday, represented a law and order group known as the Citizens Safety Committee. They were organized to rid the county of a lawless element of politicos, along with some cattle rustlers known as "the cowboys." Earp's career as a lawman is controversial because the opposing faction had a large number of supporters who despised him and his organization.

But one thing should be remembered: all the Earps were shot from behind, while their victims were plugged in front. That says a lot about who were the good guys and who were bad.

Partisans on both sides of the Pleasant Valley War, pitting cattlemen against sheep men, agreed that the best man with a gun in that feud was Jim Roberts. He might never have taken sides, but some of the Grahams stole his prize horse. He rode with the Tewksburys during the most violent days of the war before becoming a lawman in Yavapai County. Roberts had his last gunfight in 1928 in Clarkdale when two desperados held up a bank. They tried to make their getaway in a car, but Roberts stood his ground and put a bullet through the driver of the speeding auto. Old Jim was nearly seventy at the time.

When the Arizona Rangers were organized in 1901, Burt Mossman agreed to a one-year enlistment as captain. Modeled after the famed Texas Rangers, Mossman's rugged men rode the Arizona Territory, breaking up the last of the large outlaw gangs.

(Left) Pearl Hart, who robbed one too many stagecoaches in 1899, was captured, tried, and sent to the Territorial Prison at Yuma, where she immediately became one of the most popular inmates.

(Above) Most of the desperados were white males, but Apache marauders sometimes were brought to court, too. In this group, one was sentenced to hang, and the others drew prison terms ranging from ten to thirty years.

In a desperate effort to bring law and order to Arizona Territory, the Arizona Rangers were formed in 1901 under Captain Burt Mossman. (Right) A band of the Rangers, shown about 1903, prepare to ride out after the bad guys. (Below) One of the prime targets of the Arizona outlaws was the stagecoach, which usually carried money or valuables and was an easy target. This one, a Modoc coach, ran from Tucson to Tombstone.

Arizona Historical Society, Tucson

Captain Mossman's last hurrah as an Arizona Ranger was the daring capture of the notorious Augustine Chacon, a dark, handsome outlaw who boasted of killing fifteen Americans and thirty-seven Mexicans during his career. He'd been captured and sentenced to hang at Solomonville, but, just before the sentence was carried out, he escaped and hightailed it to Sonora.

Mossman persuaded Burt Alvord and Billy Stiles, two ex-lawmen turned outlaws, to arrange a meeting with Chacon in exchange for leniency. Posing as a rustler on the lam, Mossman got close enough to the cagey Chacon to get the drop on him. He brought back his man, and this time the hanging took place on schedule.

Knowing the Mexican government would be furious when the details of the capture below the border became known, Mossman resigned from the Rangers and headed *east* until the heat was off.

Now, *that's* a twist!

Finally, there's the tale of Maricopa County Sheriff Carl Hayden, best known for serving in the U. S. Congress longer than any other person in history (fifty-seven years). Few people remember Hayden's role in the capture of two train robbers in the desert south of

36   Arizona Highways Album

McLaughlin Collection

(Right) One of southern Arizona's most respected Arizona Rangers was Bisbee's Johnnie Brooks.

(Far right) The theory flourished in Arizona Territory that public hangings helped to deter potential criminals from their foul deeds. This execution of a young murderer in 1889 was the first hanging in Globe. The crowd must have found the victim's anguished expression haunting their memories for decades to come.

Maricopa in 1910. It was at Maricopa that he borrowed a Stoddard-Dayton automobile from its owner, J. F. McCarthy, who was drafted into service as the chauffeur.

The powerful car raced across the trackless desert and caught up with the Woodson brothers, known as the "beardless boy bandits," after their horses played out. Hayden ordered the robbers to surrender, but one refused to drop his pistol. So Hayden walked fearlessly toward the young man who, after a long moment, put up his hands. Only then did Hayden pocket his *unloaded* revolver.

It's the first recorded incident of a posse pursuing outlaws in an automobile. Yep, the twentieth century had at last reached Arizona.

MARSHALL TRIMBLE, *a contributing editor to* Arizona Highways, *is without a peer as a story-teller, balladeer, and popular historian of Arizona. As Director of Southwest Studies for the Maricopa County Community Colleges, he has a respected position in academia, as well. A prolific author, his latest book is* Roadside History of Arizona.

Arizona State Library

Arizona State Library

Those Who Came Before
Continued from page 14

churches as San Xavier del Bac in southern Arizona. Near San Xavier in 1776, a Spanish military outpost gave birth to Arizona's oldest major city — Tucson.

But it was not until the third decade of the nineteenth century that intrepid mountain men like James Ohio Pattie, Pauline Weaver, and Joseph Walker came to trap beaver and guide explorers across what was then northern Mexico. Other storied characters came soon thereafter — Kit Carson, Bill Williams, Antoine Leroux, and their comrades — to bring the beginnings of Yankee civilization to this wilderness.

America's fervent belief that God had ordained the United States to rule over all the land between the Atlantic and Pacific oceans — "manifest destiny," it was called — drove this nation to war with Mexico in 1846-48. When that uneven struggle was over, Mexico was forced to cede California and the Southwest — fully a third of its national territory — to the United States. New Mexico Territory was created in 1850, comprising what is now New Mexico and Arizona.

In 1853, crusty old General James Gadsden, seeking additional land for a southern railway to the Pacific, was authorized to purchase from Mexico the part of modern Arizona that lies south of the Gila River. The purchase price was ten million dollars, considered exorbitantly high by opponents of the deal.

The lure of gold brought hordes of adventurers to Arizona's desert streams and wooded mountains just before the outbreak of the Civil War. Although few were able to strike it rich, many remained to become ranchers, businessmen, farmers, and gamblers.

The first Arizona Territory was actually a creation of the Confederate States of America. It was brought into being on February 14, 1862 — exactly fifty years before Arizona became the forty-eighth state of the American Union. Confederate Arizona comprised the southern halves of today's New Mexico and Arizona, and its capital was Mesilla, near Las Cruces, New Mexico.

That fledgling territory had a short life. On February 24, 1863, President Abraham Lincoln turned his attention from Civil War strategy long enough to sign the bill creating a separate Arizona Territory of the United States, its extent essentially the same area as that of our present state.

Within a decade, Congressional Delegate Richard McCormick was pleading the case for Arizona statehood before the leaders of Congress. But that plea would go unheeded for nearly half a century.

Arizona's first territorial capital was established at Camp (later Fort) Whipple in January, 1864. That post, established only a few weeks before to protect gold seekers, was initially in Chino Valley, eighteen miles north of what is now Prescott. Tucson, Arizona's largest community and the logical site for the seat of government, was passed over because it was thought to possess Southern sympathies.

So Territorial Governor John Goodwin chose the Yavapai County wilderness, first in Chino Valley and then at the Granite Creek camp named for historian William Hickling Prescott.

Arizona's capital was spirited away by Tucson in 1867, but Prescott won it back in 1877. Only twelve years later, in 1889, booming Phoenix was able to wrest the capital away from Prescott, this time permanently. No wonder Arizona's territorial government was called "the capital on wheels."

Until the mid-1870s, while fierce Apache raiders kept settlers in some parts of Arizona in constant fear, population growth in the territory was discouragingly slow. The 1870 census showed only 9,658 Arizonans. But the flood tide of immigration was just beginning. Arizona's population soared to 40,440 by 1880. By that time, settlers were streaming in from Utah, and other pioneers were arriving from the East.

When Apache leader Geronimo surrendered in 1886, ending the Indian threat for all time, immigration accelerated rapidly. Even the most optimistic Arizonans were delighted when the 1890 census count

40 Arizona Highways Album

Mountain men, Army forts, soldiers, and their families—all are a part of the rich tapestry of early Arizona history. (Upper left) Modern Arizonans are reminded of fabled mountain man Bill Williams when they visit his monument at the community of Williams. (Above) Fort Whipple, now a Veterans Administration hospital, was a cavalry post that defended the territorial capital at Prescott. (Right) Fiorello La Guardia (second from right), later one of New York City's most famous mayors, was a cornet player in the La Guardia family orchestra in 1896. His father was at that time bandmaster at Fort Whipple.

came in, showing the population had reached 88,243.

It was during the decade of the 1880s that Arizona started to shed its image of the "Wild West" and to make mature demonstrations that it was ready for statehood. The Southern Pacific Railroad crossed southern Arizona, and soon thereafter the Atlantic and Pacific (now the Santa Fe) traversed the northern part of the territory. The fabled "Thieving Thirteenth" Legislature of 1885 mirrored Arizona's new social consciousness. A mental hospital at Phoenix was established. And a university at Tucson and a normal school at Tempe were created.

Copper became Arizona's premier metal, surpassing gold for the first time. Irrigated farming made the Salt

For years, pioneers of little Phoenix in the Salt River Valley had to depend for news on The Arizona Miner *in Prescott and the Tucson journals. (Left) By the late 1880s, however, Phoenix had the Phoenix Daily Herald as a local news medium. (Below) Arizona Territory was entering the modern world, but there were some evidences in 1890 that Arizona still had a way to go. These water merchants in Bisbee had a profitable business, and many citizens of other towns still were without a central water supply.*

Arizona State Library

McLaughlin Collection

River Valley bloom and ushered in Phoenix as the rising star of Arizona cities. Telephones and electric power brought modern civilization to Arizona communities.

As the 1890s approached, Arizona's predominantly Democratic populace chafed under the political rule of governors appointed from afar by Republican presidents. Territorial status became more and more demeaning, and Arizonans began to demand statehood with increasing stridency.

Arizona Highways Album   43

Arizona was becoming downright civilized by the 1890s, and signs of growth and development were everywhere. Geronimo's surrender in 1886 had ended the Apache threat to settlement, and the cities and towns were boasting such advanced conveniences as sewer systems and telephones.

(Left) Volunteer fire departments, such as this one at Tombstone, provided both community service and fraternal associations. (Above) Arizonans liked to brag to friends in the East about the warm winter weather, even as they do today. This shirt-sleeved gentleman filmed this message in 1893 as a Christmas card. (Right) There were no Boy Scout troops in Phoenix in 1894, but this military-minded "Boys Brigade" group served the function. One boy was berated after the photo was taken for being out of uniform.

Arizona Historical Society, Tucson

44   Arizona Highways Album

McLaughlin Collection

McLaughlin Collection

Arizona Highways Album 45

Chapter II
Into a New Century

The nineteenth century was slipping rapidly away, and frontier Arizona was fading into the mists of history, as future-oriented dreamers planned strategies to bring the territory into the Union of states. It was a fascinating period, this turn-of-the-century era, when yesterday lived side by side with tomorrow. Visitors from the East found Arizona Territory's quaint mining camps and small-town main streets a source of perpetual interest. Typical was this street at Kelvin, in Pinal County. Note the standard mix of commercial establishments here: one general store flanked on either side by a saloon. Arizona Historical Society, Tucson

Arizona Historical Society, Tucson

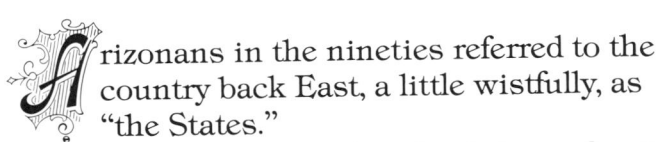

Arizonans in the nineties referred to the country back East, a little wistfully, as "the States."

Most of them had ventured to the Arizona frontier quite recently from "the States," which many regarded as stuffy, overcivilized, repressive, and completely unresponsive to the aspirations of the energetic West. But rare was the Arizonan who did not yearn to see his raw territory granted equality in that hallowed Union of American States.

Delegations left Arizona for Washington almost annually to plead for statehood, and, on several occasions, a group of Congressmen would arrange a junket to Arizona for a close-up look at these uncouth pounders at the Union door.

In 1891, despairing of acceptance by any other means, the territorial legislature authorized an Arizona constitutional convention to write a statehood charter for submission to Congress. Seventeen Democrats and five Republicans met in Phoenix during September of that year and hammered out a populist constitution that passed the U. S. House of Representatives, but was buried by the Senate.

Arizona settled back for another long wait.

Like a gangling adolescent, Arizona was a startling mixture of untamed muscle, soaring optimism, childish playfulness, and mature wisdom as the territory approached the dawning of a new century.

The Easterner's conception of the territory as a vast wasteland populated mostly by cowboys, Indians, Mexicans, Mormons, and rattlesnakes was hard to change, but Arizonans were working at it.

The intrepid Rough Riders, who covered themselves with glory while fighting under Colonel Theodore Roosevelt in Cuba, brought favorable national publicity to Arizona in 1898. So did President William McKinley's 1901 visit to Phoenix for a parade and to the Congress Mine for a demonstration of gold extraction. (Mrs.

Continued on page 52

Arizona State University Library

McLaughlin Collection

48 Arizona Highways Album

McLaughlin Collection

Arizona Territory was an amazing mix of proud cultures and lifestyles at the turn of the century: the Native American, the Hispanic, the immigrant European, a few Blacks and Asiatics — along with the rambunctious cowboy, the God-fearing Mormon farmer, the underground miner, and the elegant gambler. To many residents of the staid East, this diversity represented a strange chaos and made Arizona a doubtful candidate for statehood.

(Upper left) How, they asked, was one to make a thoughtful citizen out of a wild cowhand like this one on the Greene Cattle Company ranch in Santa Cruz County? (Center left) Unfamiliar customs, such as the Mexican funeral rituals in Clifton, were hard to understand. (Lower left) How could we absorb the Indian culture, represented here by these venerable Apache scouts at Alchesay? (Above) There was considerable doubt, too, about a new state populated by such creatures as Gila monsters.

Arizona Highways Album 49

Territorial politicians were hard at work preparing the road to Arizona statehood before the new century arrived. (Above) The Twentieth Legislative Assembly of 1899 was the last to meet before completion of the capitol building in Phoenix. Henry Fountain Ashurst (front, center, holding his hat) was to become one of Arizona's great U.S. senators. (Upper right) The 1901 visit of President William McKinley and his wife focused national interest on Arizona's statehood aspirations. He rode triumphantly in a Phoenix parade (hatless, in carriage facing camera) and later (lower right) the McKinleys visited the Congress Mine near Wickenburg. The President is in center of photo at left of the ore car. Within a few months, the President was dead, victim of an assassin's bullet.

Sharlot Hall Museum

McLaughlin Collection

Desert Caballeros Museum

Arizona Highways Album 51

Arizona State University Archives

Continued from page 48

McKinley was presented a gold bar as a memento.)

Newspapers in Phoenix and Tucson carried dispatches received by telegraph from all over the world: the latest battles of the Boer War; news from the new American possessions of Hawaii, the Philippines, and Puerto Rico; and efforts of southern state legislatures to stamp out Negro voting.

In 1900 the advertising columns of Arizona newspapers were crammed with plaudits for patent medicines that claimed to cure everything from the unmentionable ailments of women to impotency in men. One long-running advertisement offered a complete set of false teeth for $5; another, men's wool suits for $3.75.

Urban life in Arizona was becoming much like that in small cities across the nation. There were electric lights, streetcars, theaters, and golf courses. Real estate developers lured home purchasers to fashionable new subdivisions, even as they do today. Horseless carriages were beginning to appear.

But it was a different story in the rural areas, where life was still primitive and the amenities few. The backyard privy and the town water wagon were staples of life; women slaved from dawn to bedtime on household chores and child rearing; and most men did manual labor that left little free time for anything beyond a church or lodge meeting.

Arizona's economy was based on copper mining and cattle ranching in those infant years of the twentieth century. But irrigated farming was gaining fast, and increasing numbers of people were earning their living from manufacturing, retail trade, and the new tourism industry.

At Globe and Miami, Clifton and Morenci, Jerome, Bisbee, Ajo, and a dozen other rugged copper mining camps, recent immigrants from Europe toiled in stifling tunnels or in vast pits, grinding out a living and dreaming of a better future for their large families.

Continued on page 73

52   Arizona Highways Album

Arizona State Library

Arizona Historical Society, Tucson

Arizona was rapidly becoming civilized as the century turned. (Upper left) Tempe's Territorial Normal School students are shown at Old Main. Fred Irish (center, front, with bow tie) organized the male students into a cadet corps for potential military service at the time of the Spanish-American War of 1898. (Top) Created by the "Thieving Thirteenth" legislature of 1885, along with the Normal and the University, was the Territorial Insane Asylum in Phoenix. Its original $100,000 appropriation far exceeded that of the two educational institutions. (Above) The University of Arizona at Tucson was taking shape on the desert east of town, and already dreaming of academic excellence.

Arizona Historical Foundation

Arizona State Library

The Victorian Age was coming to a close, but gingerbread architecture and elaborate ceremonies were still with us. (Above) Phoenix High School occupied this charming structure about 1900. (Left) The town turned out for a parade, especially when the white-helmeted Phoenix police marched in smart array. (Facing page, upper left) A favorite Phoenix cultural center was the Dorris Opera House, a symbol of central Arizona's yearning for the finer things of life. (Upper right) The Victorian Maricopa County Courthouse looked down on the Phoenix streetcar line along Washington Street. (Lower left) The Pinal County Courthouse at Florence, still a tourist attraction today, was a masterpiece. (Lower right) So was the ornate Gila County Courthouse at Globe.

Arizona Historical Foundation

McLaughlin Collection

Arizona State Library

Arizona State Library

Arizona Highways Album 55

Arizona's Swing to Liberalism

By James W. Byrkit

On September 6, 1901, a half-crazed anarchist fired two bullets into the stomach of President William McKinley. Eight days later, McKinley died and Theodore Roosevelt became the twenty-sixth President of the United States. This marked the beginning of a new era in American life.

Roosevelt's "progressive" presidency signaled a fifteen-year decline in popular support for business and industry and a rise of national sympathy for labor, farmers, and other working-class people. This benevolent attitude toward liberal interests during the years 1901 to 1917 derived from a popular discontent many normally conservative Americans were feeling toward business. Liberal thought benefited from the backlash that had developed as a result of monopolistic and other corporate abuses of the late nineteenth century.

Throughout the nation, in the press, and on the streets; in city councils, state legislatures, and the Congress, progressives went after the city bosses, robber barons, sweatshop owners, and the adulterators of food and drugs.

In Arizona Territory, even more than across the nation, the progressives enjoyed a phenomenal popularity during this period. Before 1900 the Arizona mining industry—sponsored and directed by large eastern-based corporations—had effortlessly influenced Arizona politics and society, making the territory a virtual industrial colony. But such progressive territorial governors as Alexander O. Brodie, appointed by Roosevelt in 1902, and Joseph H. Kibbey, appointed by Roosevelt in 1905, disturbed the absolute control that the corporations had enjoyed for two decades.

By 1908, middle-class and working-class Arizonans had become a political force in the territory. They dominated the 1910 Arizona Constitutional Convention, producing a document that conservatives all over the nation found radical and deplorable.

The history of Arizona shows clearly that power politics and special interest groups, such as mining and the railroads, were not new to the state during the early twentieth century. In 1863, Arizona became a territory for many of the same reasons it later became a state: so that special interests might have more political control over the region's affairs. In the 1860s, mining people such as Charles Poston, Sylvester Mowry, and Sam Heintzelman had urged Congress to give Arizona territorial status so they could protect their investments.

Tax laws, corporation laws, labor laws—these and others cut into the money-making success of the corporate owners. It was business management's unpleasant chore to secure a political atmosphere in Arizona favorable to the corporations.

Territorial Governor Nathan O. Murphy, a Benjamin Harrison appointee in 1892, supported a mine profit tax. Many bills were introduced in the legislature to effect Murphy's request; all were defeated. In 1901, Murphy again asked for a tax on mining; again the tax failed.

But in 1902, Arizona power politics began to take a new direction. The liberal turn would last about fifteen years. That year Brodie, a member of Roosevelt's famed Rough Riders, was appointed territorial governor by his former commander. Well liked in Arizona, Brodie held many of Roosevelt's progressive attitudes. New hopes rose in the breasts of Arizona's liberals.

In 1907, the mining corporations faced the greatest effort ever launched to tax them. A new governor, Kibbey, aroused public sentiment enough to start a battle. Intent on gaining greater tax equalization, Kibbey continued to insist on heavy taxation of Arizona's mines. The corporations denounced him as an "agitator" aligned with the radical element.

Continued on page 62

Few Arizonans in 1900 complained about the mining magnates' political clout, or even about working conditions in the mines and smelters. Copper brought prosperity to the territory, and that was the important consideration. But Arizona politics took a liberal turn soon thereafter. The mine unions insisted on fewer hours, better pay, more safety precautions. (Above) Ben Williams, at left, a developer of the Copper Queen Mine at Bisbee, and bearded James Douglas (for whom the neighboring city is named) prepare to take visitors into the mine with candles and lanterns. (Right) Smelters at key locations in the territory transformed the ore into copper. You can almost feel the heat, smell the molten metal, and hear the din.

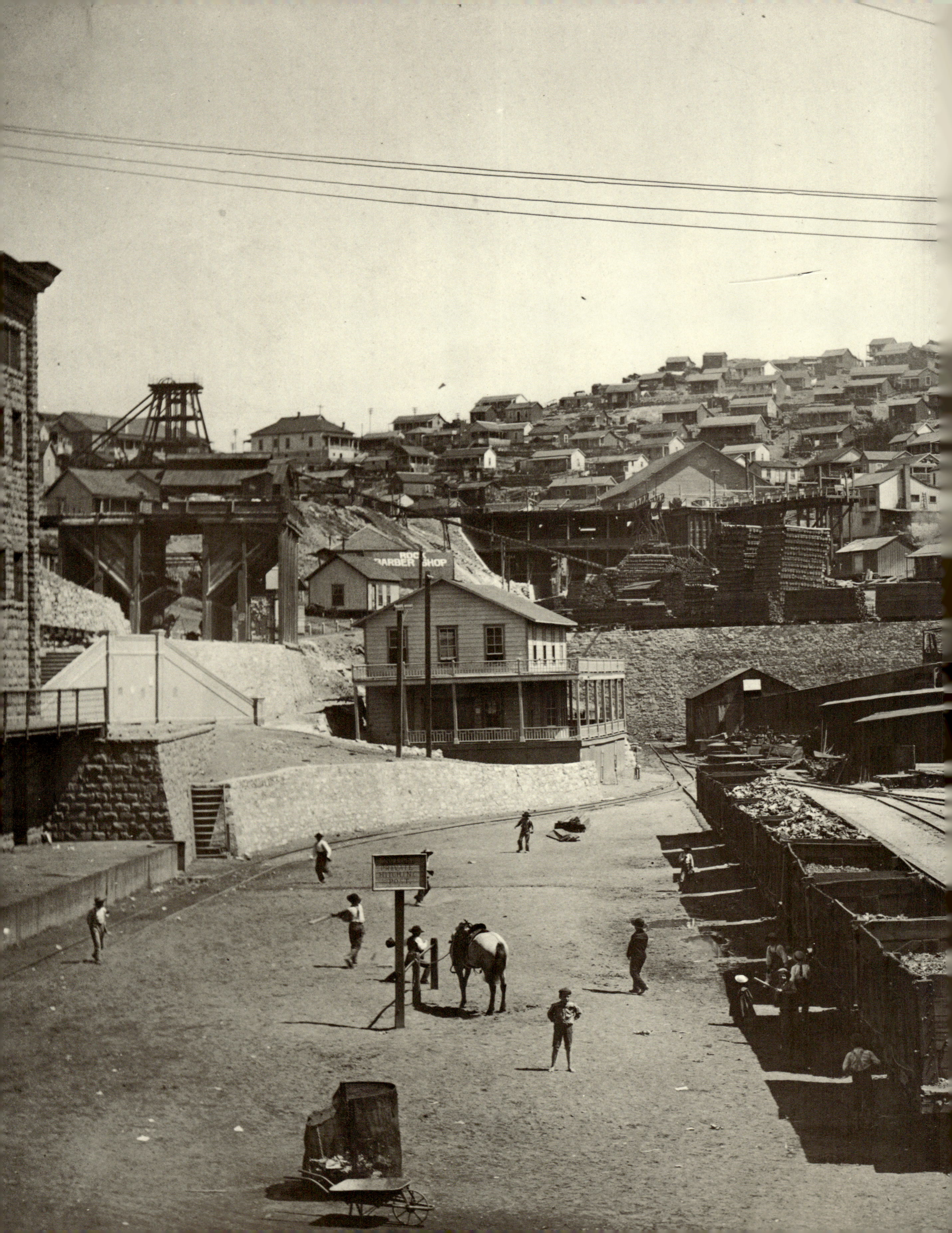
ROCK
BARBER SHOP

McLaughlin Collection

Mesa Southwest Museum

Little houses perched precariously on surrounding hills were home to the miners and their families in dozens of Arizona Territory camps. There was little concern about air quality. If the smokestack wasn't belching pollution, people weren't eating. (Left) There wasn't a tree in sight, and not much greenery of any kind, but folks in Morenci, in far eastern Arizona, were proud of their town. (Top) In Jerome, where the town was built on an almost vertical hill, merchants prospered when the miners were working overtime. (Above) Little mines all over the territory were supplied by burro trains such as this one heading for the Superstition Mountains east of Mesa.

Arizona Historical Society, Tucson

Arizona Highways Album 59

While the politicians pleaded for statehood, hard-working Arizonans went about their business as always. Early in the twentieth century, machinery was starting to relieve the back-breaking labor on the farm. (Above) On this alfalfa farm near Pima, in Graham County, a hay baler turned out beautifully square bales. (Left) No, this isn't a dish to receive television signals, but a pioneering (1904) solar energy device that focused the sun's rays and powered an irrigation pump on a farm near Tempe. (Upper right) Good old-fashioned muscle power was used to fell trees near Flagstaff in 1900, before chain saws were invented. (Lower right) The twentieth century brought few changes to the business of feeding cowboys. It was hard to improve on the chuck wagon.

Arizona Historical Society, Tucson

Arizona Historical Society, Flagstaff

Sharlot Hall Museum

Arizona Historical Foundation

Continued from page 56

After two years of this pressure from the corporate leadership, Kibbey retired in 1909. He was replaced by Judge Richard E. Sloan, an appointee of President William Howard Taft and a friend of the conservatives.

However, following the example of their national counterparts, Arizona's Democratic leaders had pledged to pursue liberal objectives in the territory's 1908 election. Arizona's labor groups combined with other noncorporate interests, declaring their ambition to be in control of the mining companies. Although the Democrats lost to Taft in the national election, they won in Arizona.

For the first time ever, the liberals controlled the territorial legislature. They immediately launched new efforts to achieve statehood.

Apart from the popular sentimental longing for sovereignty, the strongest drive that motivated most Arizonans in their movement for statehood was the desire to tax the mines, railroads, and even the few big stockmen. Arizona citizens resented seeing the profits from their mineral wealth and from exorbitant railroad rates going back East.

The public rush to liberalism left Arizona corporations politically impotent. One corporate official wrote: "I consider it of the highest importance that immediate consideration should be given the subject of the organized liberals in Arizona." He observed that "the rapid changes that are occurring in the political situation east" had helped create the adverse political climate for Arizona copper companies.

62 Arizona Highways Album

McLaughlin Collection

By July, 1910, Arizona's "radical" movement was in full swing. In Jerome, in May, the Socialist Party candidates captured two of eight offices in the city election, losing several others by narrow margins. In the next few years, Arizona Socialists and liberal Democrats won many more public offices throughout the state. Unimpressed by Republican or corporate pleas for conservatism, voters drifted leftward, away from their former position supporting big business. Fuming, the big companies sat by and watched the liberals take over Arizona politics.

On July 11, 1910, a labor union group convened in Phoenix to decide what provisions Arizona labor should demand in the new constitution.

After some debate, a long list of liberal proposals

As Arizona Territory matured, more of its citizens were able to earn their living indoors, in business and professions. (Upper left) Ross Drug Store on Cortez Street in Prescott sold drugs—period. (Lower left) There was more variety at M. Goldwater and Bro., which had department stores in Prescott and Phoenix in 1900. Barry Goldwater's father, Baron, is second from right. (Above) Banks were a bit more formidable in those days. Bearded William Christy of the Valley Bank of Phoenix was not a man for small talk.

Arizona Highways Album 63

was drawn up. These demands included measures for popular sovereignty, equal suffrage, employer liability, direct election of U. S. senators, authorization of state seizure of property, public payment of court defense costs, short terms for elected state officials, and other progressive guarantees. Also high on the list were measures barring injunctions against strikes.

The laborites felt that the two major political parties would find these provisions unacceptable, so Bisbee miners urged the formation of a Labor Party. Democratic leader George W. P. Hunt, fearing the crippling of the party by the loss of the labor constituency, persuaded Arizona Democrats to endorse labor's constitutional goals if labor would pledge its support to the Democrats. A deal was made, and thus labor came to dominate the constitutional convention.

On the day of the election of convention delegates, September 12, 1910, the liberal victory was overwhelming. One Arizonan commented that the body of the constitutional convention "was distinctively a radical organization."

Progressive-minded, anti-corporate, liberal politics characterized the Arizona State Legislature from 1912 to 1916. During this period, liberals enacted laws that provided for the eight-hour day, women's suffrage, the right to picket, recall of judges, better and safer working conditions, and other legislation that enraged corporate interests. In particular, the progressives enacted taxation laws distasteful to the mining industry.

By 1916, the copper corporations were so frustrated that the mining company managers, previously often at odds with each other, organized in a counteroffensive against the state's liberals. By 1918, the Arizona liberal movement was dead.

Business and the professions were thriving. (Upper left) The Lount Ice Plant helped make Phoenix summers bearable in the late 1890s. (Top) Lawyer J. H. Collins of Jerome kept his practice going in a tent after an 1898 fire. (Above) The Territorial Press Association was headed by Louis C. Hughes of Tucson, seated third from left. Hughes was an 1890s Arizona governor.

JAMES BYRKIT's interest in Arizona politics and labor grew out of his boyhood experiences in his native Jerome, where he developed a feeling for the social and political attitudes of Arizona's mining communities. A member of the Northern Arizona University faculty since 1973, he is a respected teacher, writer, and speaker on Arizona and the Southwest.

Arizona Highways Album 65

Prescott had lost the territorial seat of government to Phoenix in 1889, but the "Mile High City" continued to be an important mining and commercial center. Then came the disastrous fire of 1900 (left) which wiped out famed Whiskey Row and other downtown structures. (Below) Tents sprang up after the fire, and rebuilding began at once. (Facing page, left) The Bank of Arizona was a financial mainstay of Prescott and Yavapai County. (Facing page, right) Always ready for a parade or a concert, the Prescott town band posed on the board sidewalk.

First Interstate Bank

Sharlot Hall Museum

Arizona Historical Society, Tucson

Arizona Historical Society, Tucson

Arizona Historical Foundation

Benson Historical Society

Arizona's vastness and lack of roads had hampered the nineteenth century growth of the territory. But the coming of the railroads and improving of intercity highways spurred development. (Upper left) Even little towns such as Patagonia boasted fine railroad depots. (Left) St. Mary's Hospital in Tucson bought the latest in ambulance equipment in 1903. (Top) Phoenix patronized its horse-drawn streetcar service. (Above) And Benson Union High School students enjoyed their horsy school bus. No matter what the transportation, Arizona was on the move, into the twentieth century.

Arizona Highways Album 69

Arizona's worldwide reputation for fun in the sun was being shaped as early as the turn of the century. In the summer months, folks headed for the cool mountains. (Top) Excursions by train to Yavapai County sometimes were continued by buggy to pine-clad retreats. (Above) Picnics to the central Arizona foothills lured everyone from grandpa to the kids. The daring gentleman in left foreground was so informal that he removed his coat. (Right) Winter visitors enjoyed excursions into the desert. This group found what must be the granddaddy of all saguaro cacti near Fort McDowell.

70   Arizona Highways Album

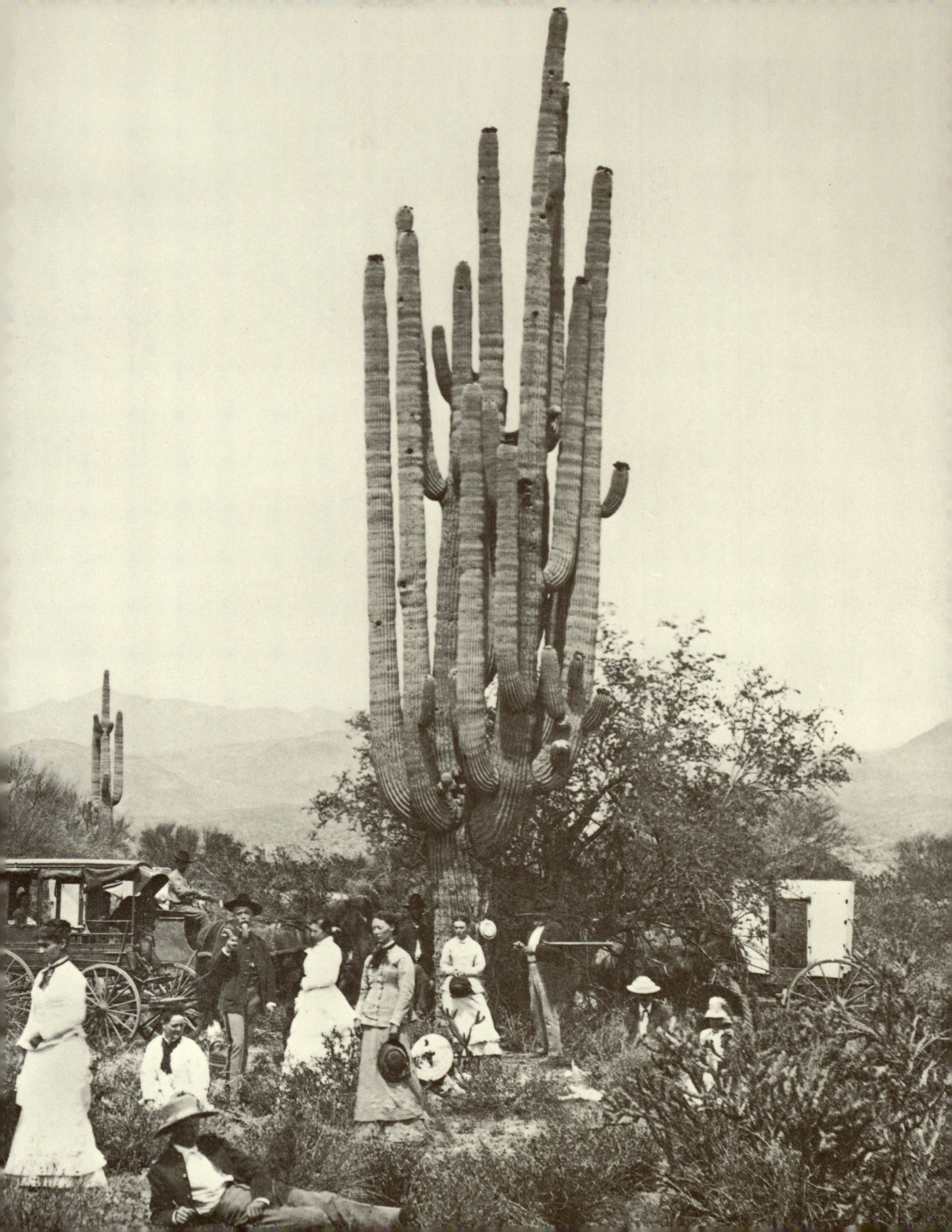

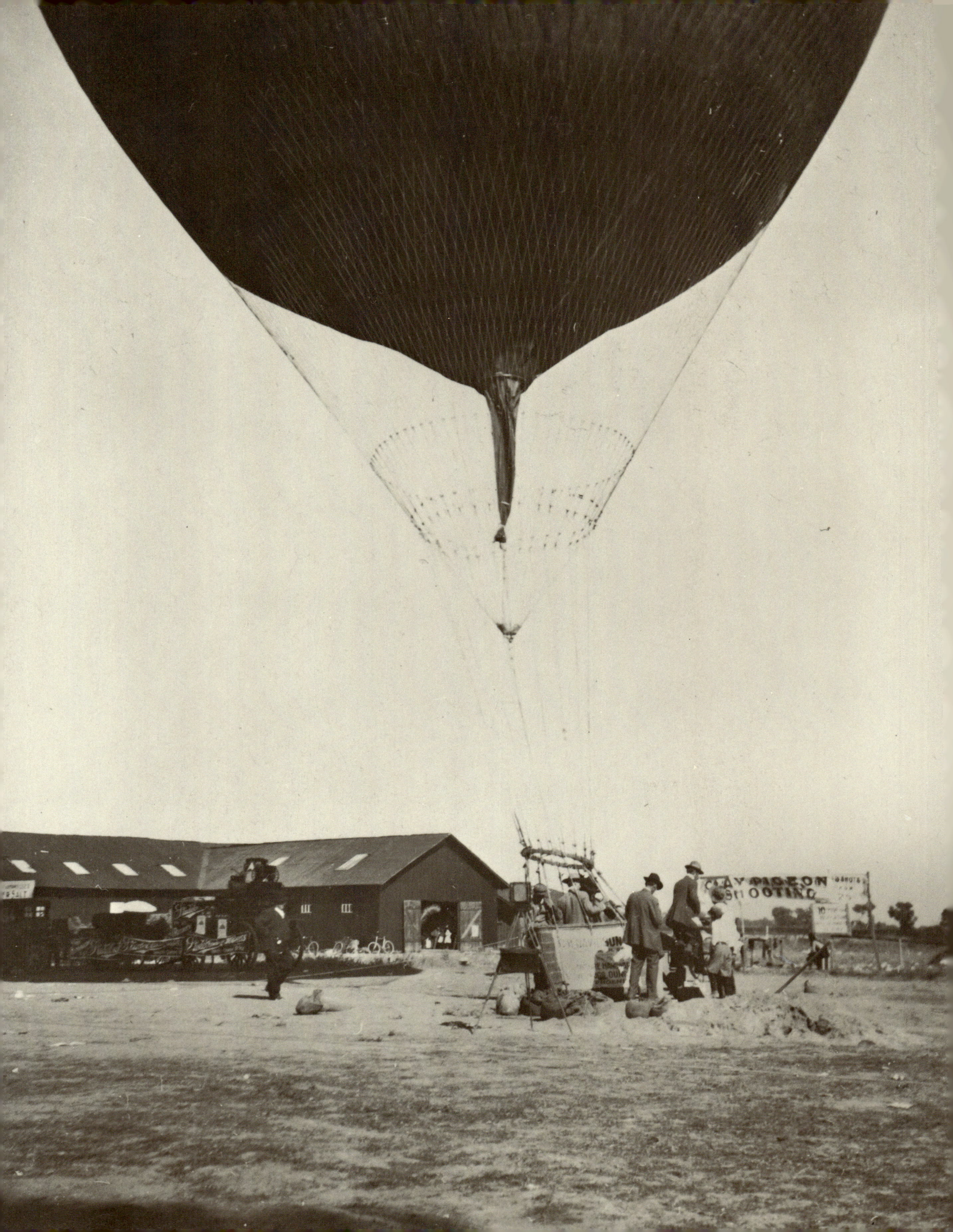
PIGEON

Arizonans found their fun in the backcountry, on the rivers — even in the air. (Left) Balloon ascensions at county fairs were a thrill for all who were brave enough. This balloon is apparently gas-filled, since no hot-air apparatus is visible. (Below) Almost every Arizona male was a hunter, and some of the ladies, too. This 1897 gathering of the Phoenix Gun Club had its counterparts in every territorial town. Arizona rifle and pistol marksmen were well known for their prowess all over the nation.

McLaughlin Collection

Into a New Century
Continued from page 52

It was the twilight of a too-brief era in the spotlight for the Arizona cowboy, whose hard, lonely life was rarely as romantic as the world believed. The territory's great ranches, some bigger than eastern states, shipped record numbers of bawling cattle to feed America. For the small rancher and farmer, life in 1900 was an exhausting struggle against the elements, predators, and unpredictable market prices.

In comparison the fortunate professional person or general store clerk was able to work indoors, in clean clothes, and for only sixty hours or so per week.

However they earned their living, Arizonans were a hardy, optimistic lot, proud of being pioneers in a new empire with a future that knew no bounds.

During rare hours away from their labors, the men loved hunting and fishing, the companionship of the saloon crowd or ladies of the evening, and such sporting events as boxing matches and football games. (The famed Carlisle Indian School football team came to Phoenix on December 31, 1899, and destroyed the Phoenix Indians, 83-6.) The women eagerly awaited community dances, desert picnics, church socials, and quilting bees.

Photos of the early 1900s show Arizonans dressed much more formally than we might have supposed. Except for cowboys, miners, and other outdoor toilers, the men are usually pictured on the streets and in offices wearing dark suits. In those stifling summer days before air conditioning, officials at the capitol and in county offices around the territory normally sweated it out, quite literally, in stiff collars and heavy coats.

And, oh, the women! Modestly garbed from chin to shoe tops in voluminous dresses and multiple undergarments, they waited in vain for the liberation that was still many decades in the future.

Churchgoing, serious about education, hungry for a taste of culture and the sciences, these Arizona frontier dwellers were hardly the uncouth hell-raisers the opponents of statehood made them out to be.

Striving toward statehood involved striving toward cultural attainments. Arizonans joined literary societies, debating groups, chess clubs, musical associations, drama troupes — anything to erase the image of the uncouth frontiersman. Such associations did much to enrich their lives. (Above) Could New York City boast a more elegant group than these top-hatted dandies of the Prescott Elks in 1902? (Left) These Tucson kids preferred riding a burro to engaging in cultural pursuits, it seems. (Upper right) Building the Phoenix Woman's Club structure was a big step forward for the ladies of the Capital City. (Lower right) In the spring, these young Tempeans' thoughts turned, not to love, but to chess.

Arizona State University Archives

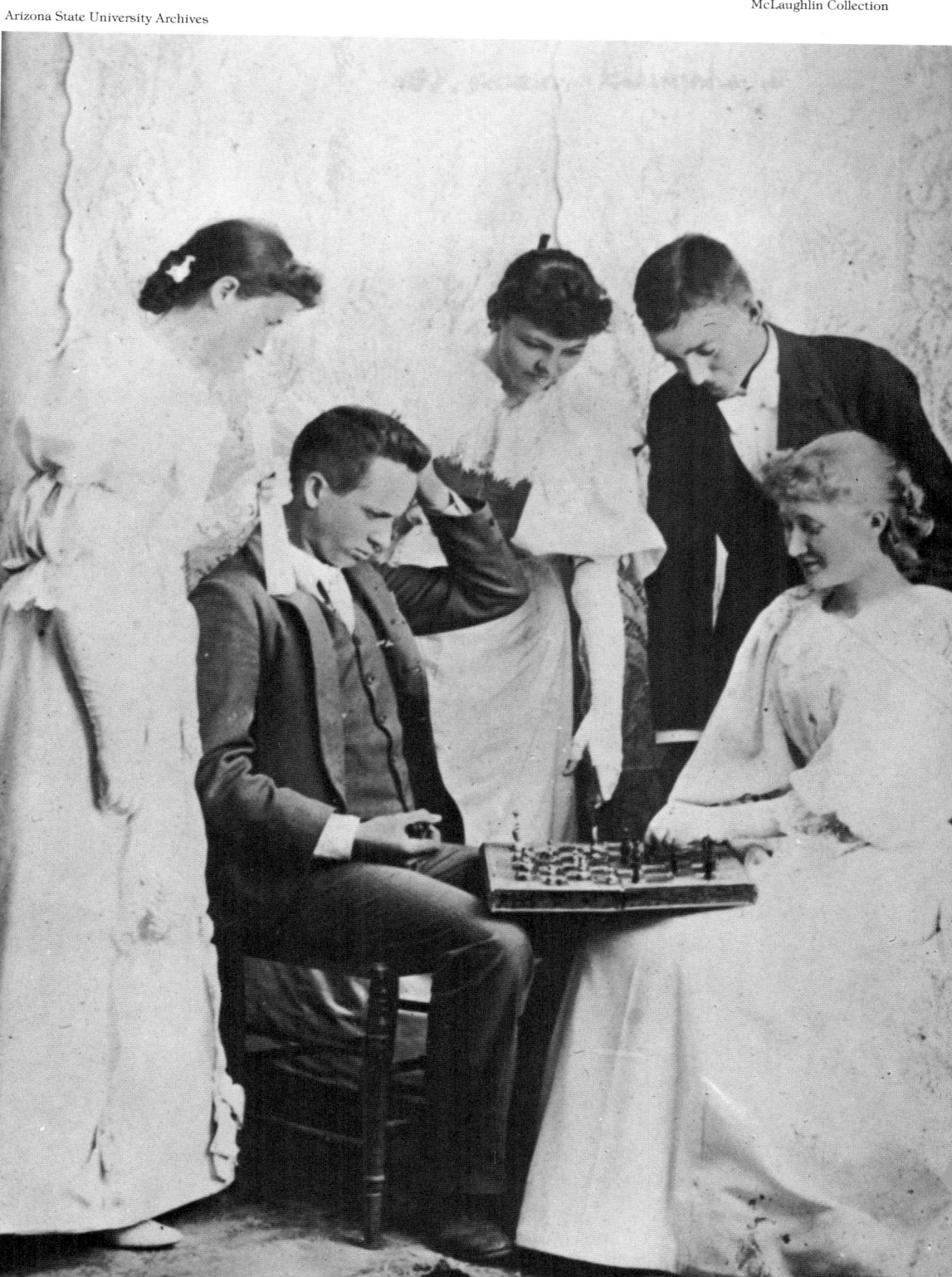

McLaughlin Collection

Arizona State Library

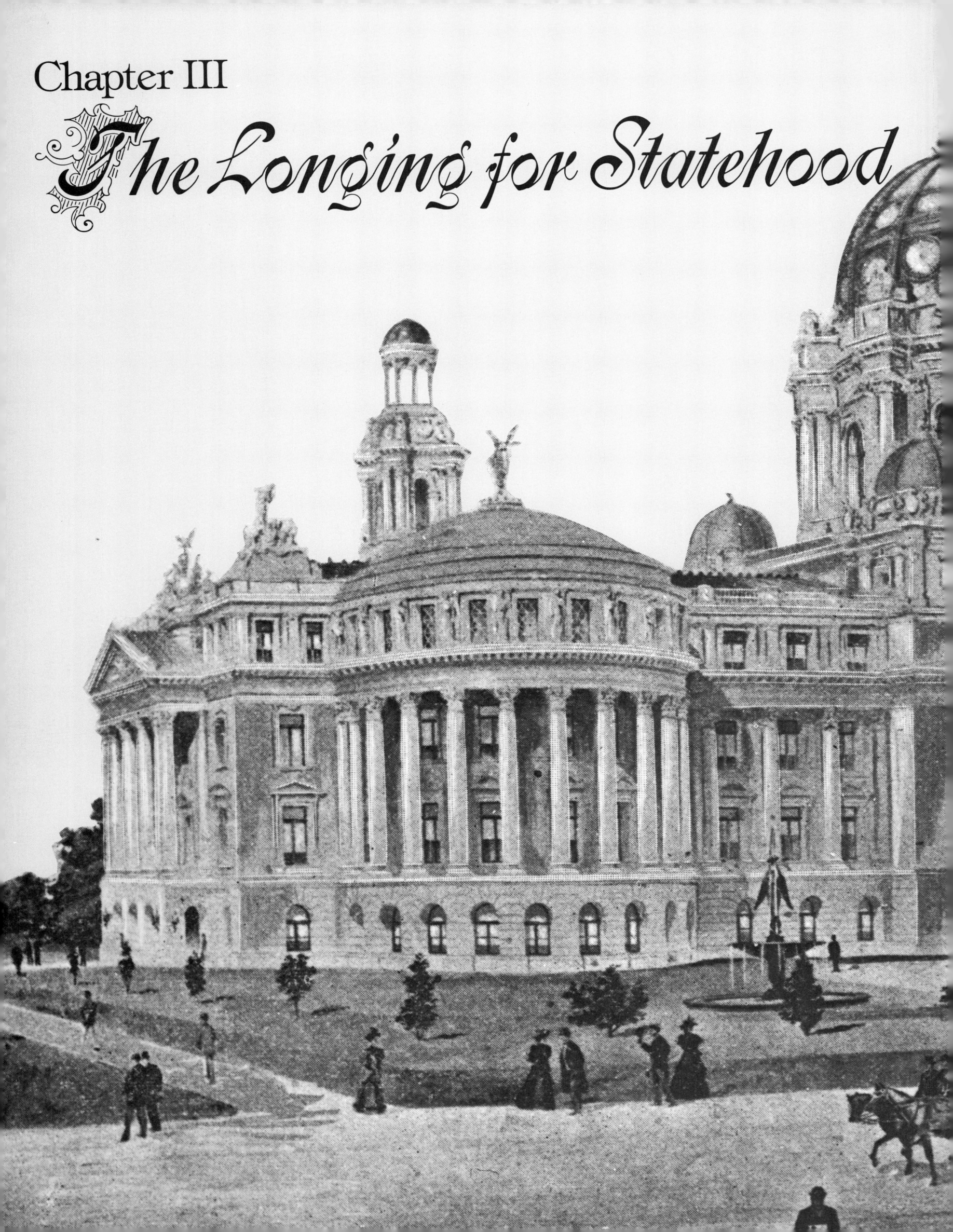

Chapter III
The Longing for Statehood

A territory aspiring to be a state sorely needed an impressive capitol building. Arizona's territorial government had been operating in city halls and courthouses, in Prescott, Tucson, and Phoenix, for decades. Then in 1899 this grand proposal for the new capitol building in Phoenix took shape on an architect's drawing board. Economic considerations prevailed, however, and this modest capitol (inset) was the building completed in 1900 on West Washington Street.
McLaughlin Collection

University of Arizona Library

The first decade of the twentieth century was an exciting time to be an Arizonan.

In addition to campaigning for statehood, Arizona citizens were conducting a small-scale industrial revolution, planning to transform the arid Salt River Valley into a garden, and linking their remote communities with all-weather roads.

Arizona's population jumped from 122,031 in 1900 to 204,354 in 1910.

In increasing numbers, women were parading in support of the right to vote. They were making it increasingly clear, in addition, that the last male bastions of sin — the saloon, the gambling hall, and the bordello — were on their way to extinction.

Although vast numbers of Americans were under the impression that the Grand Canyon of the Colorado River was a scenic wonder in Colorado, many thousands were coming to Arizona to see it for themselves. Staying on to view other Arizona attractions, they brought the word back to all parts of America that Arizona was a delightful place in which to vacation.

With the Apache problem long since solved, Arizonans turned their attention to correcting another festering impediment to statehood: Arizona's well-deserved reputation as a haven for lawlessness. Rugged old Burt Mossman, who was awed by no man alive, was chosen in 1901 to captain the new Arizona Rangers. Mossman and his tiny band of lawmen soon had the territory's notorious badmen on the run.

Probably because the rest of the nation liked to view Arizonans as rude frontiersmen, Arizonans of the century's first decade went out of their way to demonstrate their gentility. Fancy dress balls, lodge ceremonies, theatricals, and civic galas in Tucson, Phoenix, Bisbee, Prescott, and many smaller communities were every bit as sophisticated as those in comparable cities across America.

Membership was high in literary societies and musical organizations. Churches and libraries were established all over the territory, and there was remarkable interest in science and the arts. Northern Arizonans, eager to have an institution of higher learning, succeeded (1899) in establishing a normal school at Flagstaff, where the Lowell Observatory had been founded not long before. Tempe's normal school had been in operation since 1886, and the University of Arizona had been Tucson's pride since 1891.

Truly, civilization had come to Arizona's deserts and mountain country.

With all their gains — in population, industry, agriculture, tourism, education, and gracious living — Arizonans were keenly aware that something terribly important was missing. That something was the full-fledged citizenship and the sense of belonging that could come only with admission to the Union of American States.

John Irwin, an Iowan who was the last nonresident to be appointed as a "carpetbag" Arizona governor, expressed Arizona's longing for statehood as early as 1893:

> The condition of a Territory is dependence upon the National Government. That of a State is independence in all things. A Territory is in vassalage. A State is in equality, a full-grown man without a master.

So long as full membership in the Union was denied to Arizona, her people would be second-class citizens, unable to vote for president or to choose their own governor — or even to cast a vote in the Congress.

Continued on page 96

Science and technology enthralled Arizonans in the early years of the twentieth century. The University of Arizona was launching research programs, and solar energy devices were being tested in the Salt River Valley. (Above) Tucson folks marveled at barnstorming biplanes. (Right) The young lady peering into the telescope at Lowell Observatory at Flagstaff personified Arizona's fascination with science.

Arizona Historical Society, Flagstaff

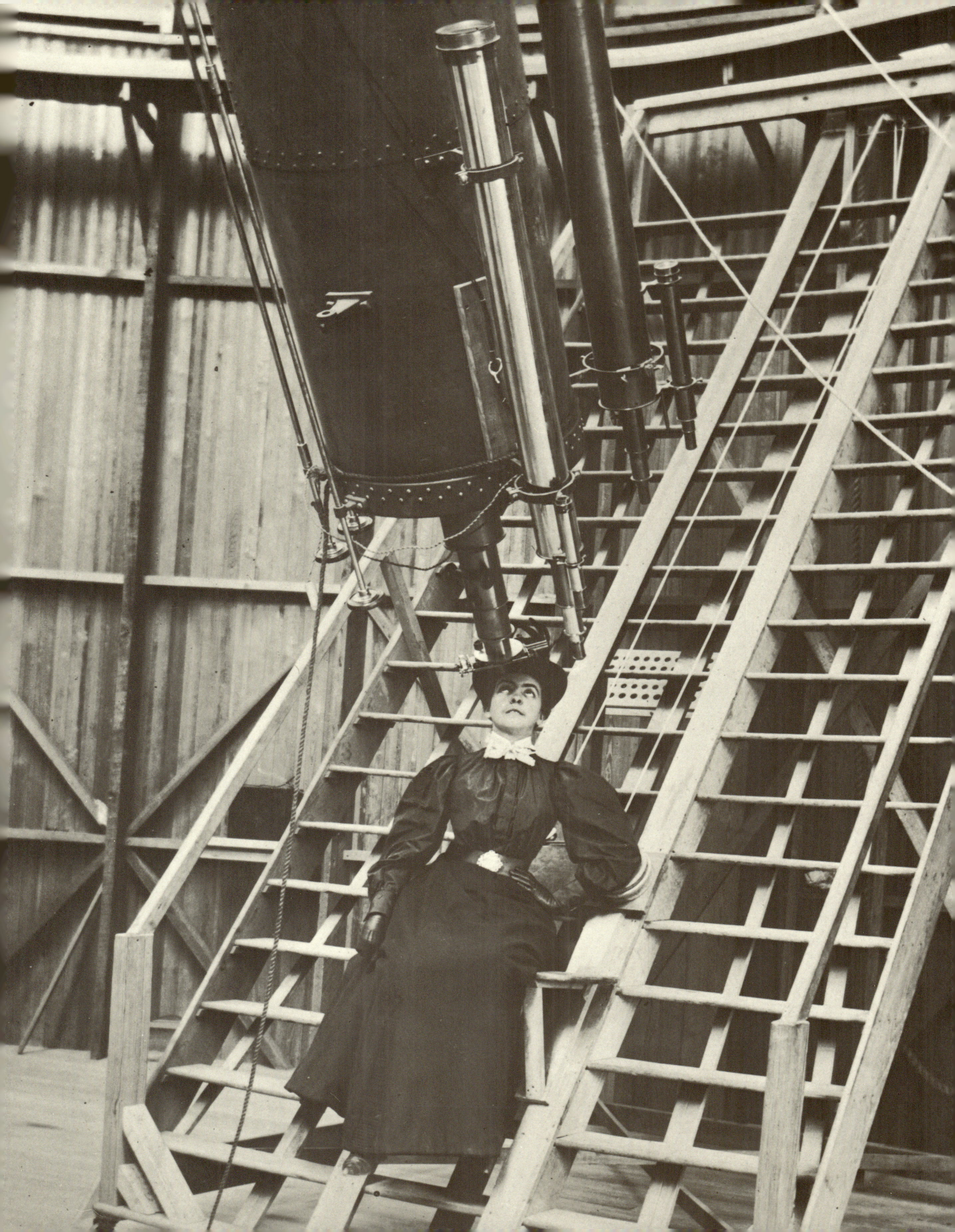

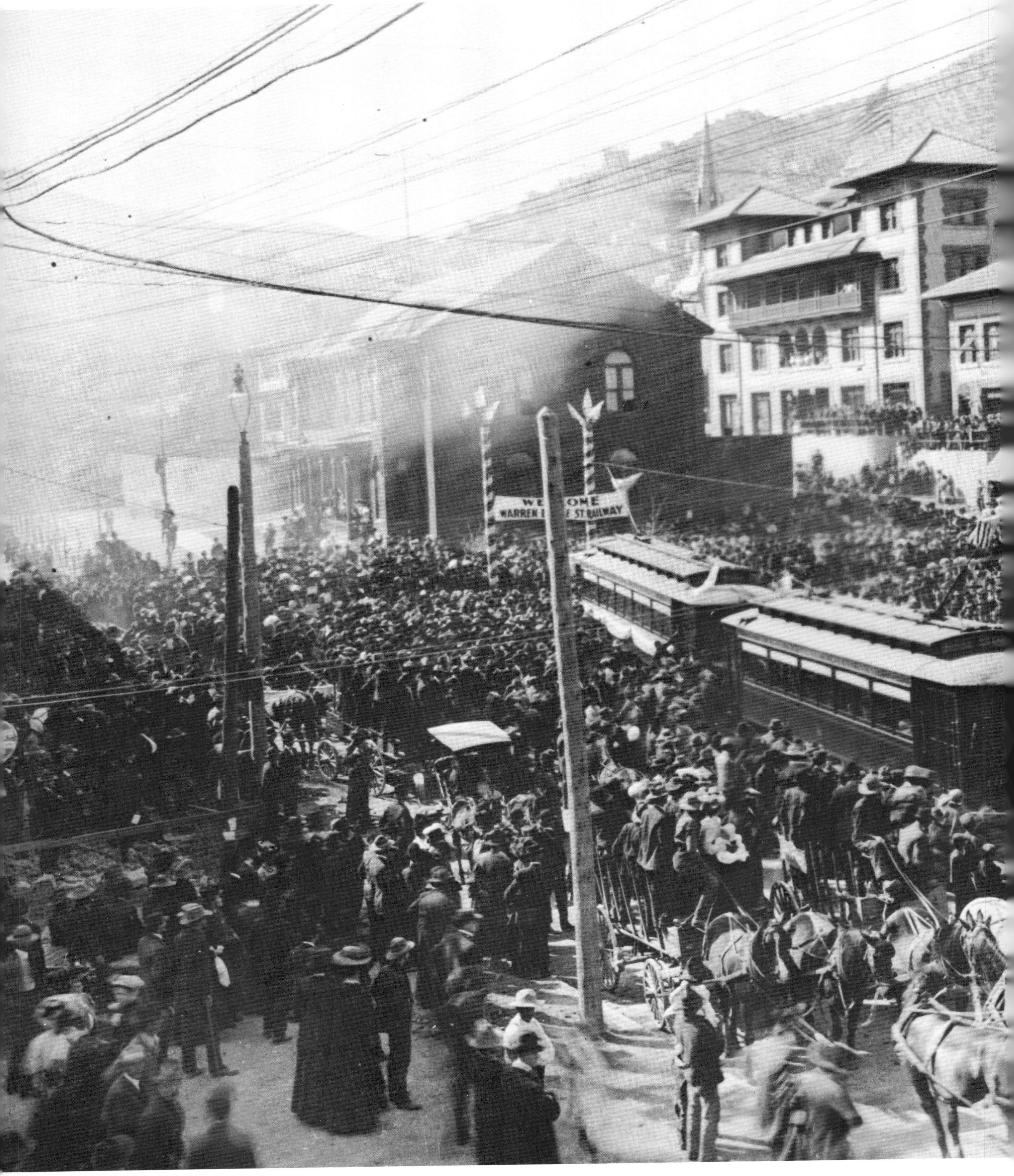
WARREN
ST. RAILWAY

Special Cut Prices On Rigs

For This Little Wagon — **$75**

THIS IS ONE OF THEM ASK TO SEE OTHERS

It is well finished, of good material and construction, has wide, roomy seat, upholstered in genuine leather, is stylish and is the biggest value in its grade that we have ever carried.

PRATT-GILBERT CO.

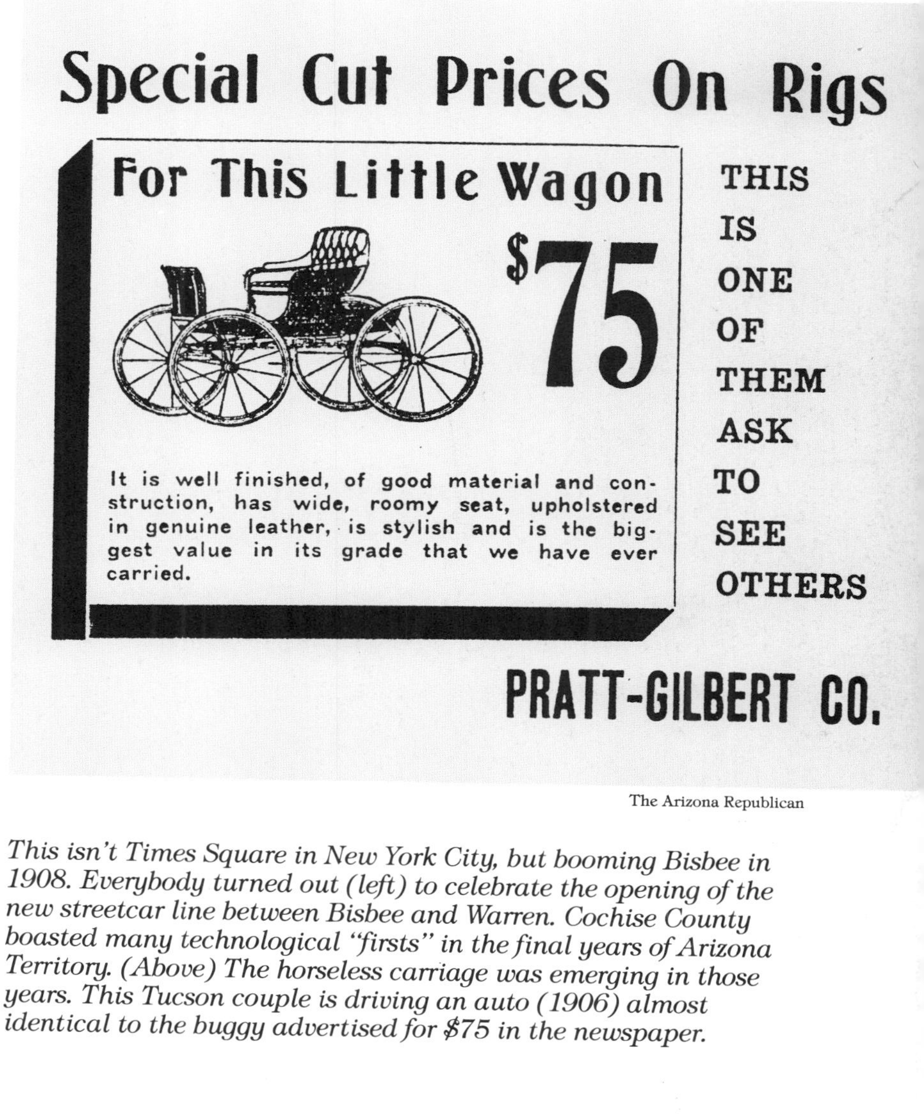

The Arizona Republican

This isn't Times Square in New York City, but booming Bisbee in 1908. Everybody turned out (left) to celebrate the opening of the new streetcar line between Bisbee and Warren. Cochise County boasted many technological "firsts" in the final years of Arizona Territory. (Above) The horseless carriage was emerging in those years. This Tucson couple is driving an auto (1906) almost identical to the buggy advertised for $75 in the newspaper.

University of Arizona Library

Bisbee Mining and Historical Museum

Arizona Highways Album 81

Senator Albert Beveridge

Marcus Smith

Early Efforts for Statehood

By Bernard L. Fontana

Although the nineteenth century had failed to bring Arizona to statehood, renewed hope came with the dawning of the twentieth. The Republican platform for 1900 asserted, "We favor home rule for, and the early admission to statehood of the Territories of New Mexico, Arizona, and Oklahoma." But Republican President William McKinley came and went from Arizona in 1901 — the year he was assassinated and succeeded by Theodore Roosevelt — without saying anything important on the subject.

President Roosevelt brought with him to the presidency the notion that the United States should be an imperial nation, one proffering colonial status on such lands newly acquired from Spain as Puerto Rico and the Philippines. Sharing this view was fellow "progressive" Republican Senator Albert J. Beveridge of Indiana, chairman of the key Senate Committee on Territories. In 1902, Beveridge and a couple of his colleagues made a whirlwind tour of Oklahoma, Arizona, and New Mexico, all being considered for statehood.

"And now comes the junior senator from Indiana with two associates from New England," former Arizona Governor Nathan O. Murphy told the *New York Times*, "who made a hurried rush through the Territories a few weeks ago in a Pullman car, hunting for adverse testimony and predetermined to report against passage of the omnibus bill [enabling statehood for the three territories], in the supremacy of their ignorance and conceit assaulting in a most vicious and untruthful manner the people and resources of two very prosperous and progressive Territories," i.e., Arizona and New Mexico.

Marcus Smith, Arizona's delegate to Congress, said he "met the committee — I never could have overtaken it — at Phoenix and it remained there one day, the longest stop in all its record so far as I know, and 'investigated' a police judge and some census enumerators, and had an interpreter with them scouring the town to see whether some Mexican could be found who could not speak English, and thus prove valuable witness for the purpose of the investigation."

The visitors paused in Tucson and Bisbee and, according to one historian, "almost omitted consideration of the great mining and irrigating enterprises, but took good care not to miss the gambling and all aspects of urban depravity....[Senator Beveridge] saw the cactus rather than the alfalfa fields, and the barren hills rather than the mines that in them lay."

The resulting report was unflattering: "Arizona is a mining camp, and the bill admitting her is gerrymandered so shamefully that if the Republicans were to carry the state by ten thousand, she would still send two Democratic Senators to Washington." Moreover, "The people must be sufficient in number; they must be on an equality with the remainder of the people of the nation in all that constitutes effective citizenship; they

Continued on page 86

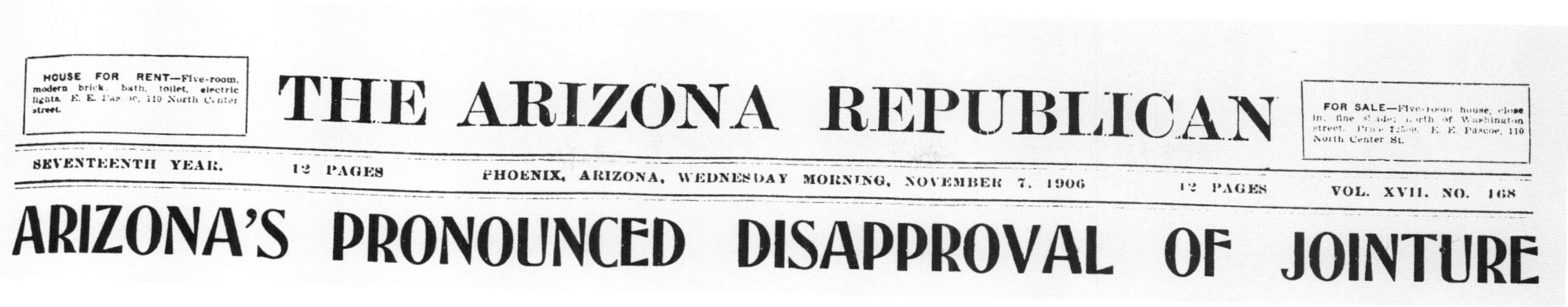

THE ARIZONA REPUBLICAN

SEVENTEENTH YEAR. 12 PAGES   PHOENIX, ARIZONA, WEDNESDAY MORNING, NOVEMBER 7, 1906   12 PAGES   VOL. XVII. NO. 168

ARIZONA'S PRONOUNCED DISAPPROVAL OF JOINTURE

Arizona and New Mexico Territories were too sparsely settled in 1903 to be granted statehood, said the political czars of the East. But Senator Albert Beveridge of Indiana (facing page, left), who chaired the Committee on Territories, had a bright idea: Why not bring them in as a single state, with the capital at Santa Fe? Marcus Smith (facing page, right), Arizona's delegate to Congress, opposed joint statehood with all his might.

Afraid of losing Arizona's identity in a joint-statehood scheme, the territory's leaders succeeded in defeating it at the polls (above) in 1906. The cartoon at right shows House Speaker Cannon and President Roosevelt trying to make up with Arizona, as joint statehood lies dead. Senator Beveridge, in the background, is cursing the election outcome. (Below) Douglas citizens celebrated by holding a formal funeral for joint statehood.

SALOON
THE CALUMET
MEDIGOVICH & NOBILE
GENERAL
MERCHANDISE.
COPPER CITY
BEER
BAZAAR
PHOTOGRAPH
GALLERY.
LOWEST PRICE
STORE
BLUE STORE
CLOTHING
MEN'S
FURNISHINGS
SHOES
THE OLD
KENTUCKY HOME
SALOON
ROOMS
BAZAAR
DRUG STORE

Visiting congressmen were impressed by Arizona's spirit, but they found the territory a little rough around the edges. (Facing page) Bisbee's Brewery Gulch offered alcoholic solace, gambling, and other pleasures. The saloon and brothel (top) at the Kofa Mine in Yuma County was popular. Jerome (above) was rough-hewn, but people dressed up for funerals.

Arizona's youthful tourism industry was beginning to make itself known in the late territorial years. (Below) Tour groups, dressed as for a formal reception, visited the Casa Grande Indian ruins near present-day Coolidge. This ancient "apartment house," more than seven centuries old, is still a tourist mecca. (Right) W. J. Murphy's Ingleside Inn, east of Phoenix on Indian School Road, was the Salt River Valley's first major resort hotel. Horseback riding was a major attraction for guests in 1910.

National Archives

Continued from page 82

must have developed the resources of the land they occupy; and finally have further resources susceptible of like development to bring the proposed new state up to the average of the remainder of the nation."

Thinly veiled in all this was the Indiana senator's view of "Spanish Americans"—one acquired during the 1898 war with Spain and from a visit he made to the Philippines—as being less than qualified for citizenship. He considered the refusal of some Spanish Americans to learn English to be a kind of treasonous act. And neither did he have a high regard for Arizona's Mormon minority.

Arizona politicians didn't take this lying down. Former Governor Murphy excoriated Beveridge's senatorial allies, including Knute Nelson of Minnesota, a "foreign-born member of the committee...who presumes to air his ignorance in a speech against the admission of Territories about which he knows absolutely nothing. While there is no argument in alluding to anyone personally, it is in exceedingly bad taste for the gentleman from Norway to deny freedom to any Territory, especially those he knows nothing about."

As for Senator Thomas B. Bard of California, continued Murphy, "he is quoted as having said that 'Arizona has reached its limit of development, its mines will play out, its population decrease, and it can reclaim no more arable land,' &c. I hesitated to believe it possible that a senator of the United States could either be so ignorant or so virulent as to make such a statement. If he made it, however, and I have seen no denial from him, he is guilty of little less than a crime against Arizona, as well as against his own State."

While the omnibus bill of 1902 was never voted on in the Senate, the following year the recommendation was made by Beveridge to bring New Mexico and Arizona into the Union as a single entity, one likely to fall into the Republican camp. Arizonans reacted overwhelmingly against the proposal, informing their delegate to Congress in 1903 they feared the state "might lose her name, identity, and history."

But Beveridge persisted, and, in 1904, Congress debated the jointure compromise. The Indiana senator made a stirring speech favoring "Arizona the Great," with the capital to be located in Santa Fe.

86 Arizona Highways Album

McLaughlin Collection

Suddenly, Arizonans who for years had lobbied in Washington in favor of statehood now lobbied against it. On the last day of the 1905 Territorial Fair held in Phoenix, 3,000 people signed a petition which read, in part, "We affirm that with almost no exceptions our people are unilaterally opposed to this obnoxious union .... We prefer to remain a Territory indefinitely rather than lose our identity." And the Phoenix City Council took note of President Roosevelt's tacit support of the Beveridge plan and changed the name of Roosevelt Street to Cleveland Street.

Arizonans' preferences were underscored at the end of 1906 when they formally voted against jointure by a vote of 16,265 to 3141 — quite the opposite of the vote in New Mexico, whose people saw more to be gained than lost in such a marriage.

In 1909, President William Howard Taft visited the territory and let it be known he favored statehood for Arizona provided its constitution not be like that of recently admitted Oklahoma, a state he characterized as "a zoological garden of cranks." He doubtless was concerned about the control of the territorial legislature by the "laborites" — or "socialists," as they were occasionally called — headed by "radical" or "progressive" (depending on one's point of view) George W. P. Hunt. Hunt espoused such measures as the initiative, referendum, and recall (even of judges); a state corporation commission; a state tax commission for equitable evaluations and assessments; the direct primary; and the printed ballot marked in secret.

Whatever misgivings Taft may have had, in mid-1910 he approved congressional enabling legislation introduced by Congressman Edward L. Hamilton of Michigan allowing Arizonans to elect fifty-two delegates to a constitutional convention. The stage was set for the next act in the Arizona Statehood play, among the longest running in United States territorial history.

BERNARD FONTANA, field historian at the University of Arizona Library, is a professional anthropologist as well as a historian. A contributing editor of Arizona Highways, *he is the author of many books and articles on the history and culture of Arizona and the Southwest.*

Arizona Highways Album

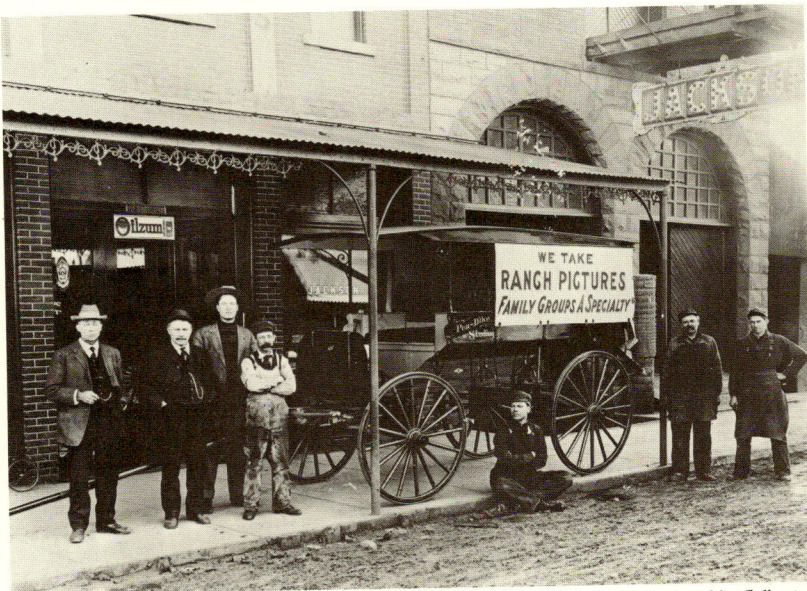

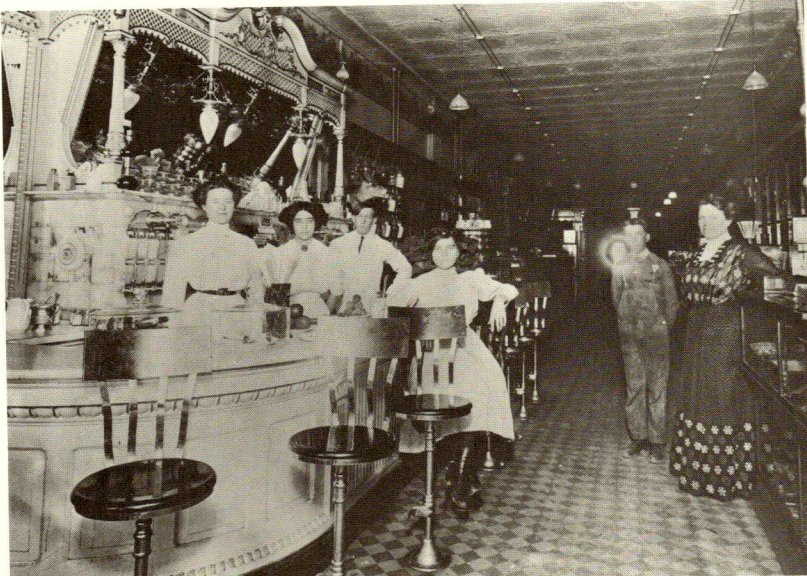

Work places were becoming modern and civilized as Arizona approached statehood. (Top) Hawkins Drug in Buckeye offered many non-pharmaceuticals, including jackknives. (Center) The Pen-Dike Studio of Phoenix roved central Arizona taking pictures of ranch families. (Above) The Shumate soda fountain was a popular Prescott gathering place in 1911. (Right) There was no air conditioning at the McKee Cash Store in Phoenix, but the ceiling fans helped cool things down a little.

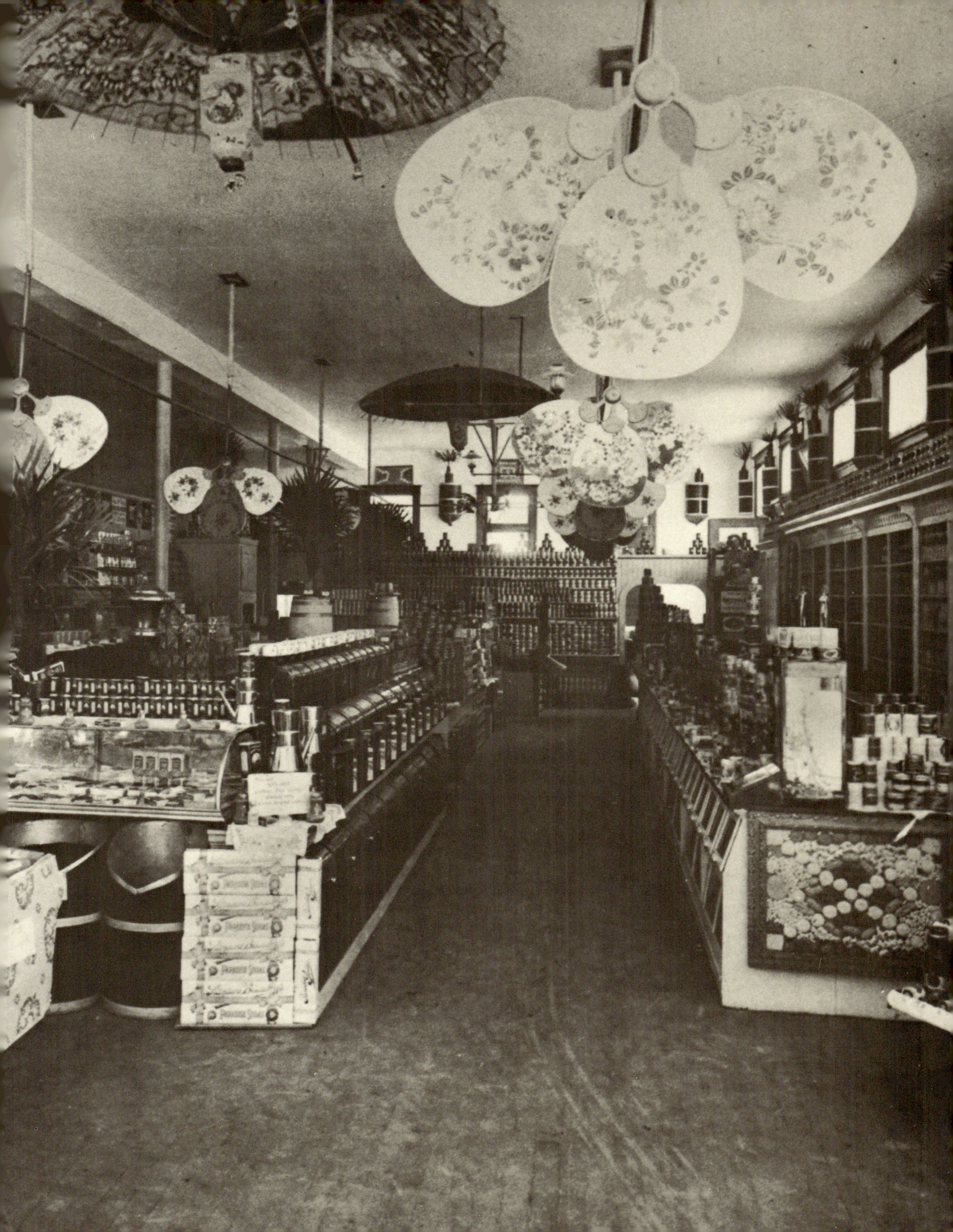

Good Old Days? Bah, Humbug!

By Maggie Wilson

During the last several decades of her eighty-six years, my mother said a gleeful "Hallelujah!" every time she tossed clothes into a washing machine.

As a housewife whose lifetime in Arizona spanned from horse-and-buggy territorial days to the three-terminal complex at Sky Harbor International Airport in Phoenix, she had, she said, "witnessed the invention of more marvelous machines than I can say grace over."

But the washing machine epitomized her own liberation from the good old days.

In her younger years in Globe, "Washdays were like moving hell, taking two loads at a time," she'd say, "and bending over that washboard was enough to put a permanent warp in a body's backbone."

Truth to tell, washdays in Arizona Territory didn't begin on washdays. They began with making the soap—a glutinous boiled mess of lye, tallow, and ashes concocted, because of the strong odor, over an outdoor bonfire.

Then there was the making of the starch, which had to be strained for lumps and scum. And the melting of the bluing balls—marble-hard little numbers used in the final rinse tub on the theory they made white clothes whiter. It must have been a little bit of washday heaven when Fels Naptha bar soap and Mrs. Stewart's Liquid Bluing became available.

Washday itself began about sunup with the chopping of wood for yet another bonfire and the carrying of water, bucket by bucket, to fill the tubs atop the fire. (As the water heated, the housewife was free to prepare a killer-sized breakfast—usually fried eggs, steak, bacon, beans, gravy, biscuits, jams, honey, and coffee. Folks didn't fret about cholesterol in those days.)

Soap and clothes were placed into the first tub to be boiled and stirred with a broom handle bleached white with use. Fished out of that brew and put into the next tub, the clothes were scrubbed on a corrugated washboard that had a tendency to take skin off knuckles as well as dirt out of clothes.

After they had been hung out to dry, freshly laundered clothes were sprinkled with water, rolled into tight little balls, and stashed in laundry baskets overnight. They were pressed with heavy flatirons heated atop the wood-burning stove. Heat control (a dampened finger flicked against the iron's sole) was especially crucial for pressing starched garments. Too hot, the starch scorched; not hot enough, the fabric stuck.

Bathing was the Saturday Night Special of the territory. More water to haul and heat on the kitchen stove. Young'uns were bathed in metal tubs in the kitchen; adults carried hot water to the bathroom's tub, using a kerosene stove to take the chill off the room in winter. (Presuming, of course, there *was* an indoor bathroom. In towns, there usually was; in the country, there usually wasn't.)

Summertimes, the living was easy. Okay, *easier*. Mexican cots were hauled outdoors for cooler sleeping. Cot legs were placed in empty jars, the better to discourage scorpions and other creepy crawlers.

"Most folks didn't wear enough nightclothes to flag a handcar," Mother recalled, "and when the fire whistle blew on summer nights,

Arizona pioneer women were amazingly resourceful. They took whatever fate gave them, which usually wasn't much, and made do with it. (Facing page, upper left) No tree at Christmas time in the desert? Decorate some tumbleweeds. (Upper right) No electricity? Chop some wood for the kitchen range and heat some water for family baths. (Center) It didn't snow often at Cochise, but when it did, you had to draw water from the well just the same. (Lower left) Baby's bath was wherever you found room for the tub. (Lower right) Ah, washday! What a difference an automatic washer-dryer would make.

McLaughlin Collection

McLaughlin Collection

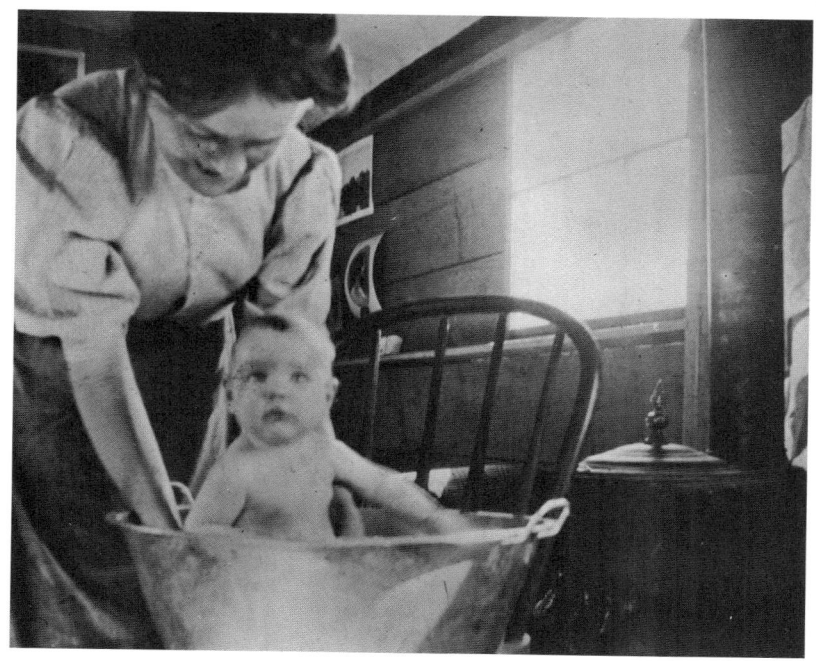

Arizona Historical Society, Tucson

Joyce Collection

McLaughlin Collection

Arizona Highways Album 91

they didn't stop to get presentable. One volunteer fireman always showed up in his longjohns, but never his false teeth."

Cooking was of the from-scratch variety, including bread baking. Frijoles (beans) were the backbone of territorial diets, served at all three meals. Staples such as flour, lard, baking powder, coffee, and sugar were "store-bought" items. Ice and milk were delivered by horse-drawn wagons in town; a dampened burlap cooler box and one's own cow were *de rigueur* in the country.

Canning, preserving, or sun-drying everything from tomatoes and berry jams to herbs were annual add-on chores during spring and summer months. But "feckless" was the word for a housewife who didn't keep a vegetable patch, some fruit trees and berry bushes, and a flock of chickens in the backyard.

As Mom recalled those days, every woman had her own area of expertise. Dressmaking, maybe, or quilting, corn growing, ham smoking, or music making. She considered her own talent to be healing the sick. Sick humans or sick horses, she meant, and often the treatment was the same for man or beast.

Her home remedies consisted of such things as turpentine, cascara, Epsom salts, calomel, castor oil, pennyroyal, glycerine, oil of cloves, cod liver oil, mint leaves, honey, whiskey, and Arizona sunshine.

"I stopped the bleeding on many an open wound with a poultice of cobwebs, saved many a horse with my watermelon seed tea," she'd proudly relate, "and cured many a miner and cowboy's diarrhea with hefty slugs of blackberry brandy."

Though she could look back in fondness at those pre-statehood years, it seemed always to be a fondness *sans* regret.

"I think we had a better sense of our own creatureliness in the scheme of things," she'd say. "We lived and worked outdoors as much as indoors. We knew the orbits of moon and stars and found solace and inspiration in glorious Arizona sunrises and sunsets. Didn't have to peek around a high rise to see them, either."

Arizona Highways Album

Arizona Historical Society, Tucson

Those were some of the positive parts of territorial life.

These were some of the negatives: "Looking back, all we women seemed to do was work, work, work. Even in slow-down times there were socks to be darned, collars to be turned, lamps to fill, wicks to trim, wood to chop, meals to prepare, dishes to wash, the garden to hoe.... It really wasn't the menfolks' fault that they didn't give us a hand around the house. Men simply didn't in those days.

"I think a lot of us suffered guilty pangs of resentment that men did their chores, or worked their shifts, and then they were done. They were free to read the paper, play some cards, go to town, and socialize in the saloons and lodge halls. Those were the days when that little poem was all too true: Man may work from sun to sun, but woman's work is never done."

Then she'd laugh, shrug, and say, "Compared to that, give me conditioned air and fabrics that wash and wear. Good old days? Bah, humbug."

MAGGIE WILSON *is a contributing editor to* Arizona Highways *and a former columnist for* The Arizona Republic. *A native Arizonan, she has never lost her awe and admiration for the state's people and places. Keen of wit and blessed with insight, she is a Phoenix free lancer who can turn a phrase with the best of them.*

(Above) While their long-suffering wives were slaving away under the most primitive conditions at home, what were the men of late territorial days doing? Why, they were toasting the ladies at the nearest saloon, safe in the knowledge that it was a sacred, all-male refuge.

(Following pages) Still, there were times when ladies and gentlemen of Old Arizona stepped out of their ordained sex roles and enjoyed each other's company. An outing at Sabino Canyon north of Tucson has been a favorite of Tucsonans for a century or more. That's Harry Arizona Drachman, an Arizona civic leader for decades, in the white shirt in the foreground.
Arizona Historical Society, Tucson

Arizona Highways Album 93

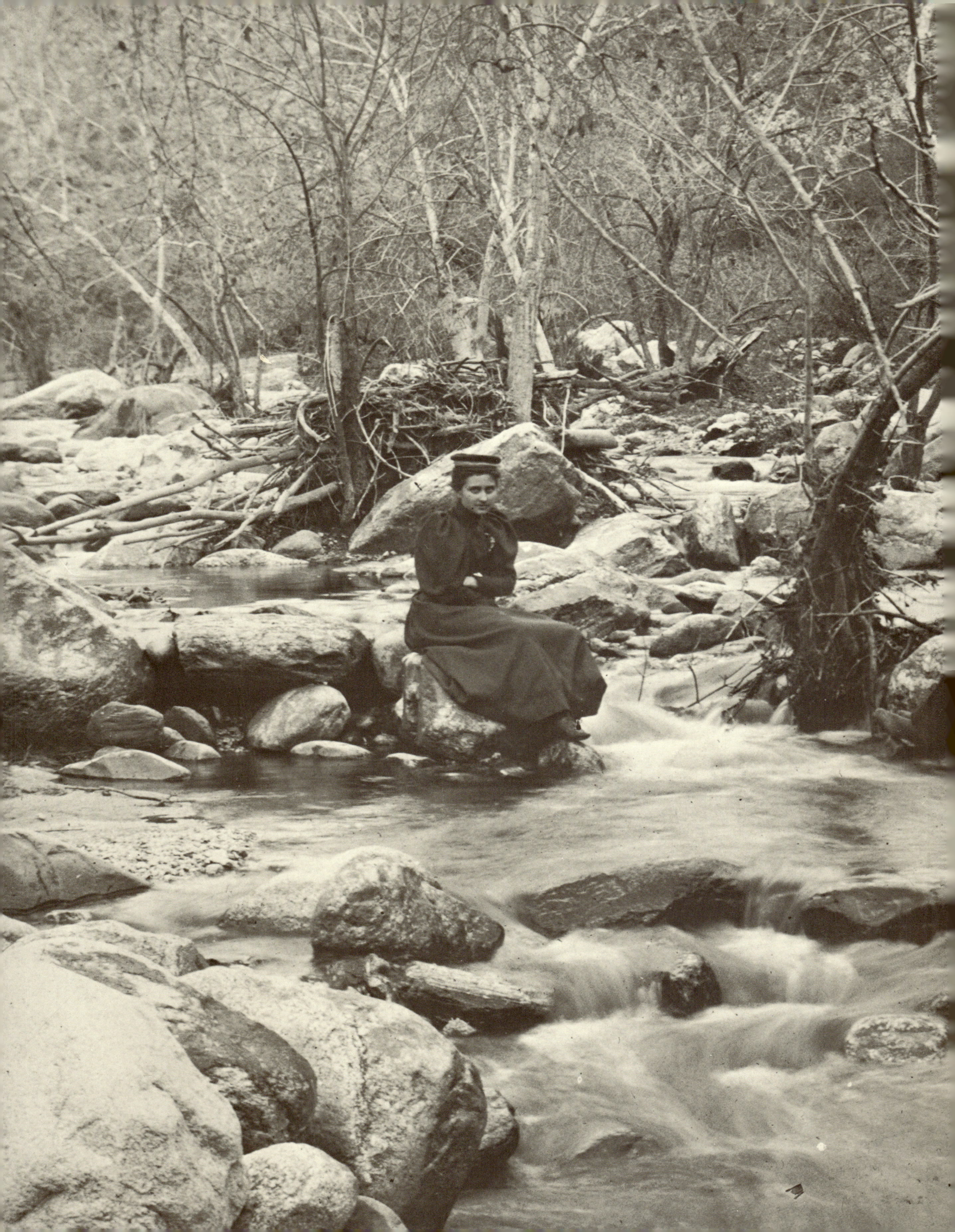

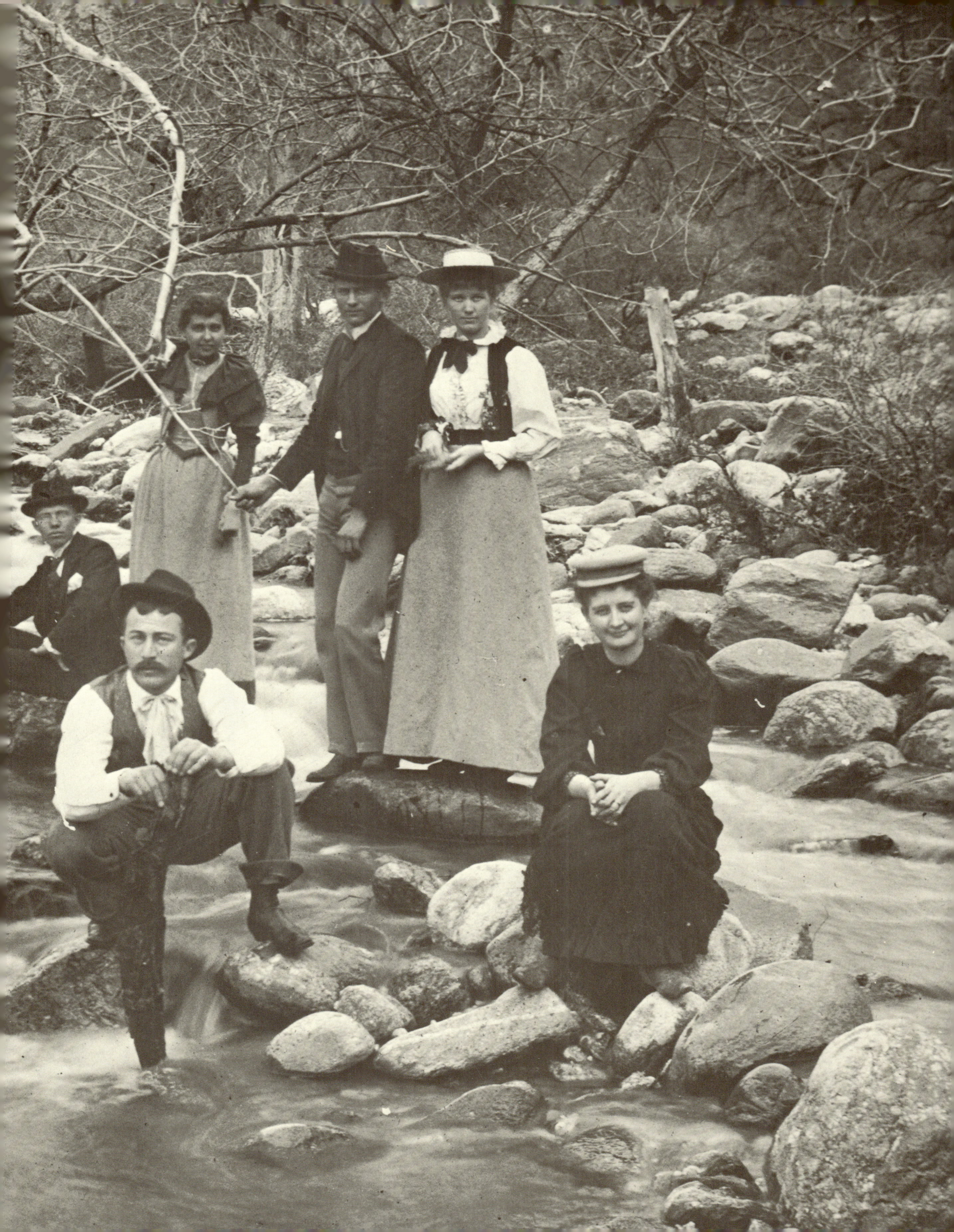

The Longing for Statehood
Continued from page 78

Arizona's angry and impatient people were bursting with the same spirit that drove the American colonists of 1776 to offer "their lives, their fortunes, and their sacred honor" in the glorious cause of independence from a distant despot.

The turn of the century brought Arizonans a bit closer to realization of their statehood dream. In August, 1900, the grand new Territorial Capitol was completed at 17th Avenue and West Washington Street in Phoenix. The legislature and territorial offices thus were able to move from borrowed quarters for the first time.

Unfortunately, the new capitol was in an area subject to flooding, as were many other sections of the Salt River Valley. Recurring inundations served to underline the crying need for control over the deadly drought-and-flood cycles of the Salt River, spurring planners to rush toward the construction of Roosevelt Dam. The establishment of the annual Territorial Fair in 1905 and laws banning gambling and prostitution in 1907 provided additional evidence of Arizona's maturity.

All this feverish preparedness for statehood was for naught, however, so long as the rest of America perceived Arizona as an uncivilized wasteland. So delegations of politicians and business leaders trekked periodically to eastern population centers to tell Arizona's story.

In 1905, a special train brought influential Congressmen to Arizona to see for themselves. The lawmakers were especially impressed by such events as the gala banquet at Metcalf, in southeastern Arizona, held in a converted mine stope illuminated by electric lights. It was served by a corps of waiters as grandly uniformed as those at the Waldorf-Astoria in New York City.

Such gestures were effective public relations ploys, but the real maturing was proceeding at an accelerated pace. New towns, new municipal services, new conveniences, new modes of transportation, and new ways of earning a living made Arizona ever more attractive to newcomers.

Despite the outrage of most Arizonans, Senator Albert Beveridge of Indiana tried to promote a plan that would have brought New Mexico and Arizona into the Union as a single state. But "jointure," as it was called, was defeated soundly by Arizona voters in 1906.

In 1907, Oklahoma became the forty-sixth state, leaving (of the active candidates) only New Mexico and Arizona languishing outside the Union's door. Then, in 1908, events began to move the dream of statehood ever nearer to reality.

Judge Richard E. Sloan was chosen as an Arizona delegate to the 1908 Republican National Convention, where he was instrumental in getting a pledge for separate Arizona statehood into the GOP platform. In November, William Howard Taft was elected President of the United States and gave his promise to support Arizona's aspirations. Republican Ralph Cameron was elected as Arizona's delegate to Congress, thus easing fears of national Republican leaders that the territory was hopelessly Democratic.

Taft visited Arizona in 1909 and was impressed with the progress he saw on every hand. He appointed Sloan as Arizona's governor, with the assurance that he would be the last governor not chosen by the people themselves. The longing for statehood was about to be satisfied at last.

Sharlot Hall Museum

Arizona State University Archives

Arizona Historical Society, Tucson

There was time for play, even in those rugged territorial days. Baseball was popular, and every little town had its team. Football was regarded by many as too brutal, and it was outlawed in scores of colleges for a time. Girls were considered too frail for most sports, but basketball was gentle enough. (Above) This Prescott High School girls' basketball team of 1906 may not have been champions, but did you ever see six prettier athletes on one squad? (Left) The Tempe Normal School football team of 1902 never got to play in Sun Devil Stadium, but they were well uniformed. (Bottom left) The University of Arizona team (not yet the Wildcats) disdained such sissy equipment as helmets.

Arizona Highways Album 97

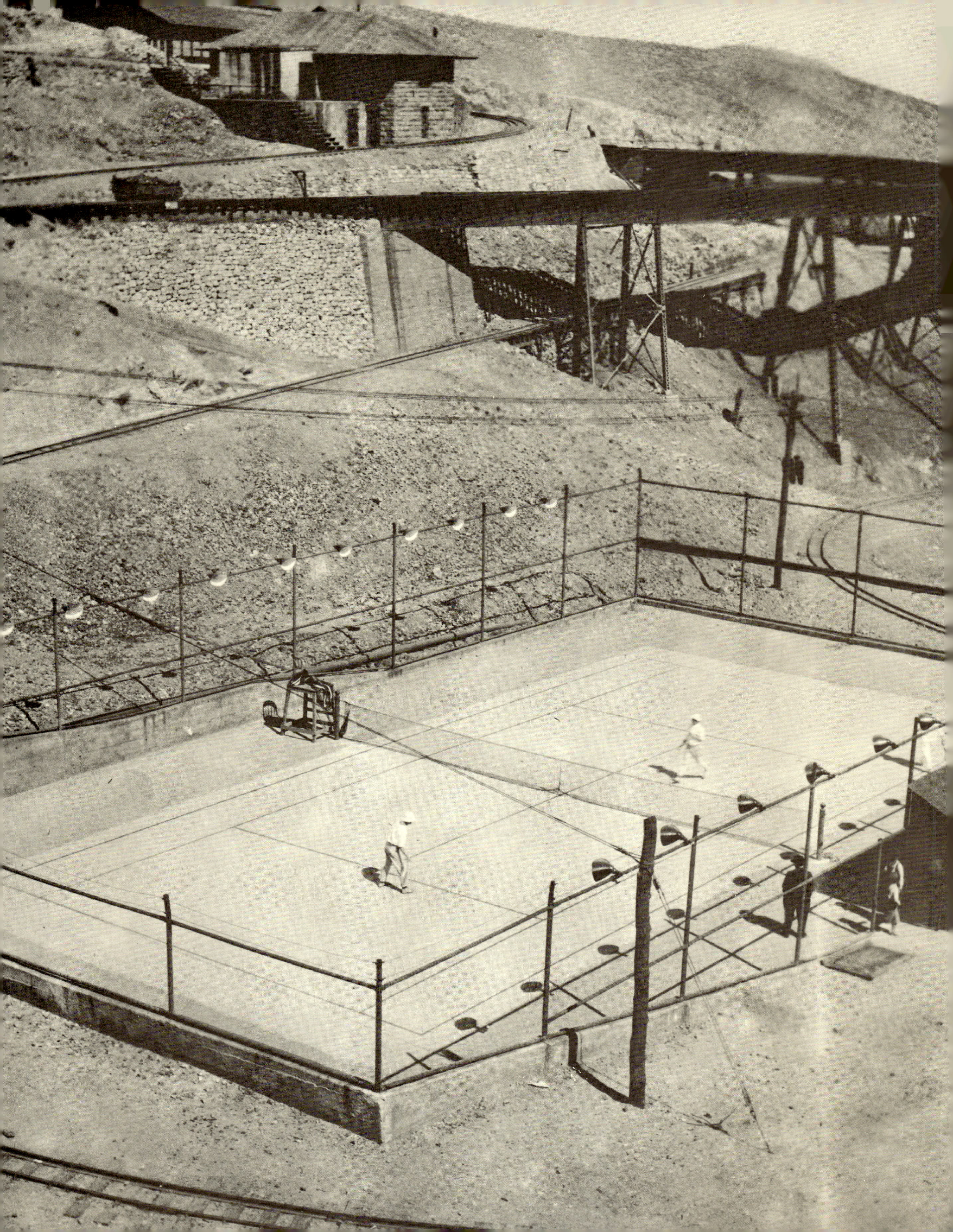

Arizona Historical Society, Yuma

Arizona Historical Society, Tucson

You took your sports fun where you found it in early-day Arizona. There were few stadiums or golf clubs, but you could get your exercise in the wide open spaces. Tennis buffs at Morenci (facing page) were lucky enough to have a lighted court in 1915. (Above) Long before author Dick Wick Hall designed his mythical desert golf course at Salome, the cowboys at Russellville in Cochise County laid out a five-hole course and rode their horses between shots. (Left) Boxing was against the law, off and on, but Yuma fans of 1912 saw Mexican Gus Livingston, left, take on Butch Allen in a well publicized bout.

Arizona Historical Society, Tucson

Arizona Highways Album

Chapter IV
Mr. Taft Says 'No'

Washington Evening Star

Washington Evening Star

Arizona's potential for greatness was grossly underrated in the final territorial years, even by her most optimistic boosters.

Territorial Governor Richard Sloan, speaking out for statehood wherever he could find a handful of people who would listen, tried hard to come up with impressive facts and figures about Arizona's development. About the best he could do was to repeat the obvious fact that "our forty-seventh state," as he always called it, would be the fifth largest in area.

In a *Sunset* magazine article, he mentioned Arizona's copper production, the growth of irrigated farming, the 2,000 miles of railroad, and the sixty newspapers and journals being published in the territory.

Then he made a prediction that had Easterners hooting in derision: "Arizona will soon support a population of well over 200,000 people."

Such extravagant claims were being made by Arizona statehood supporters in Congress, too, but they did not affect the issue much. The decision would be made, as always, by horse-trading politicians in smoky caucus rooms and hotel bars.

The Democrats in both houses of Congress usually had favored statehood for Arizona, but the Republicans had lingering reservations about admitting a bunch of wild frontiersmen who voted Democratic, favored free coinage of silver, leaned toward votes for women, and were eager to experiment with such populist toys as the initiative, referendum, and recall.

Even so, the House passed Representative Edward Hamilton's statehood enabling act (for Arizona and New Mexico) in January, 1910, and sent it to the Senate, the graveyard of Arizona's hopes on several earlier occasions. Some energetic vote swapping went on there for weeks, until at last Senator Joseph Bailey of Texas greased the skids for its final Senate passage on June 16. President Taft signed it four days later.

All Arizona celebrated with bonfires, parades, and the firing of venerable weapons that hadn't been discharged since the Apaches were terrorizing the frontier.

100 Arizona Highways Album

Washington Evening Star

For more than three decades, Arizona and New Mexico had been pounding on the Union door without success. Now, in 1910, having defeated the unpopular joint statehood plan for the two territories, Arizonans were filled with optimism that this would be the year. President Taft had given tentative approval to separate statehood—if the constitutions weren't too radical—and Ralph Cameron, Arizona's Republican delegate to Congress, was busy lining up votes. The enabling act, putting both territories on the final road to statehood, passed the House and Senate in early 1910 and was signed by Taft on June 20. Cartoonist Berryman of the Washington Evening Star *captured the expectation and elation of that historic springtime.*

Arizona Highways Album 101

(Below) Governor Richard E. Sloan was the last chief executive of Arizona Territory. Appointed to the governorship by President Taft in early 1909, Sloan spent nearly every waking hour speaking and writing on behalf of Arizona statehood. Wherever he could find a crowd such as the throng gathered to witness the annual rock-drilling contest in Bisbee (right), he spoke out for the cause.

But Arizona was not home free — not quite yet.

Only a few months before, President Taft had made his swing through the territory, warning crowds in Phoenix, Prescott, and other communities where he stopped that he would block the door to statehood if Arizona came up with a radical constitution like Oklahoma's. The bulkiest president in American history, just over 320 pounds, could certainly block any door he chose.

At the top of his list of hated constitutional provisions was recall of elected officials, especially judges. A noted lawyer and future Supreme Court chief justice, Taft could envision no end of mischief if a judge had to make decisions in the shadow of a recall threat.

"If you want to be certain that I'll veto your constitution," he told prominent Arizonans, "just go ahead and put judicial recall into it."

Continued on page 122

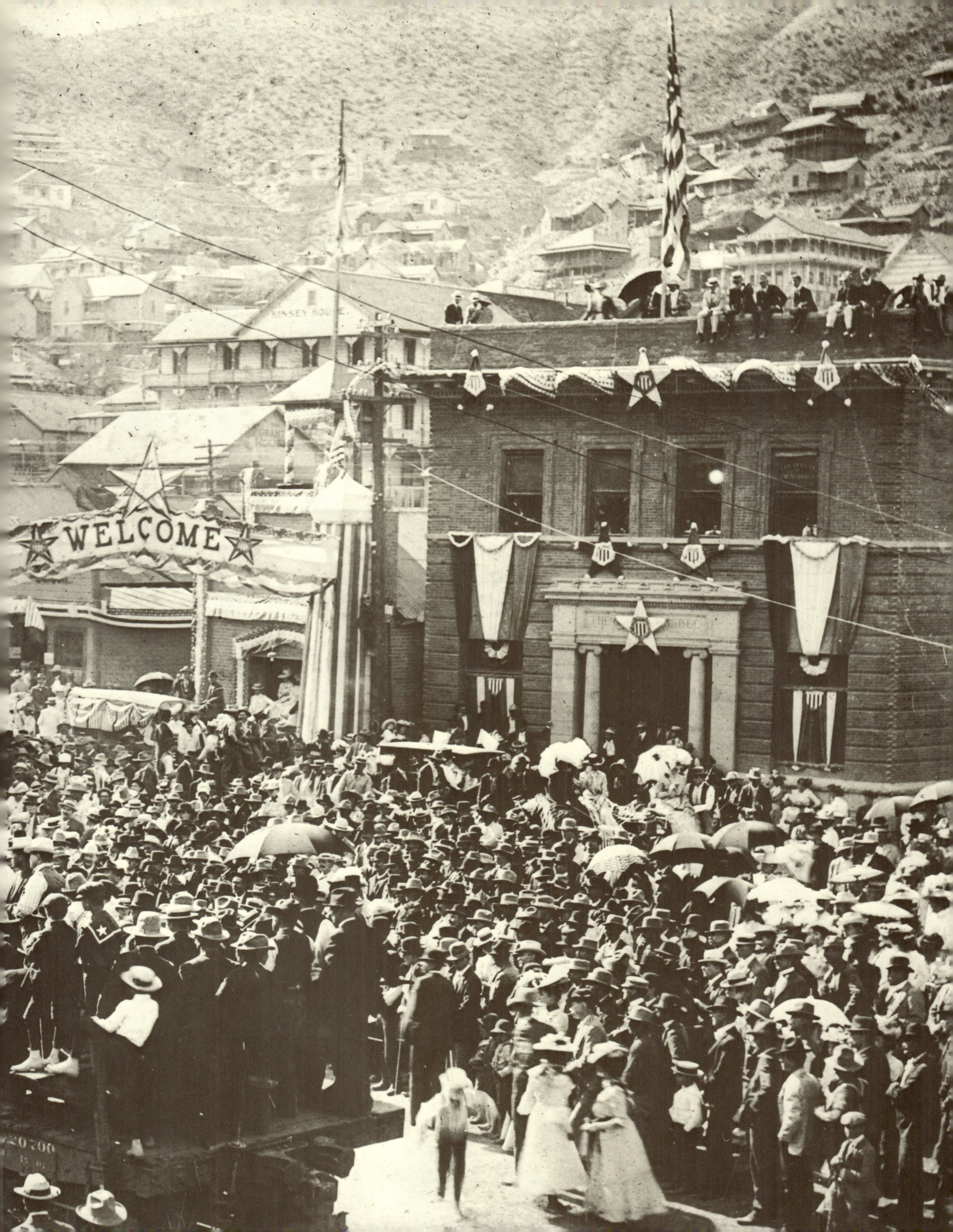
KINSEY HOUSE
WELCOME

Here's a Reason!

Statehood guarantees an extremely active demand for all kinds of Phoenix and Salt River Valley real estate next fall and winter.

Assure yourself of some of the profits that will be made by taking advantage now of the prices we are making on Suburban and Ranch Property.

Remember, this office is always in a position to aid you in financing your real estate deals.

Dwight B. Heard

S. E. Corner Center and Adams
Phoenix

The Arizona Republican

Arizona State Library

Real estate developers didn't miss a trick, even in 1910. Dwight B. Heard (top), Phoenix developer, publisher, and later candidate for governor, urged investors to get in on the coming land boom that statehood would bring. (Above) There was plenty of undeveloped land available in the Salt River Valley. Expensive homes line exclusive streets in the area just south of Camelback Mountain today, but it was open farmland in 1910. (Right) Vanished now are the charming rural drives along shady irrigation canals, where children swam and oldsters fished.

Salt River Project

104   Arizona Highways Album

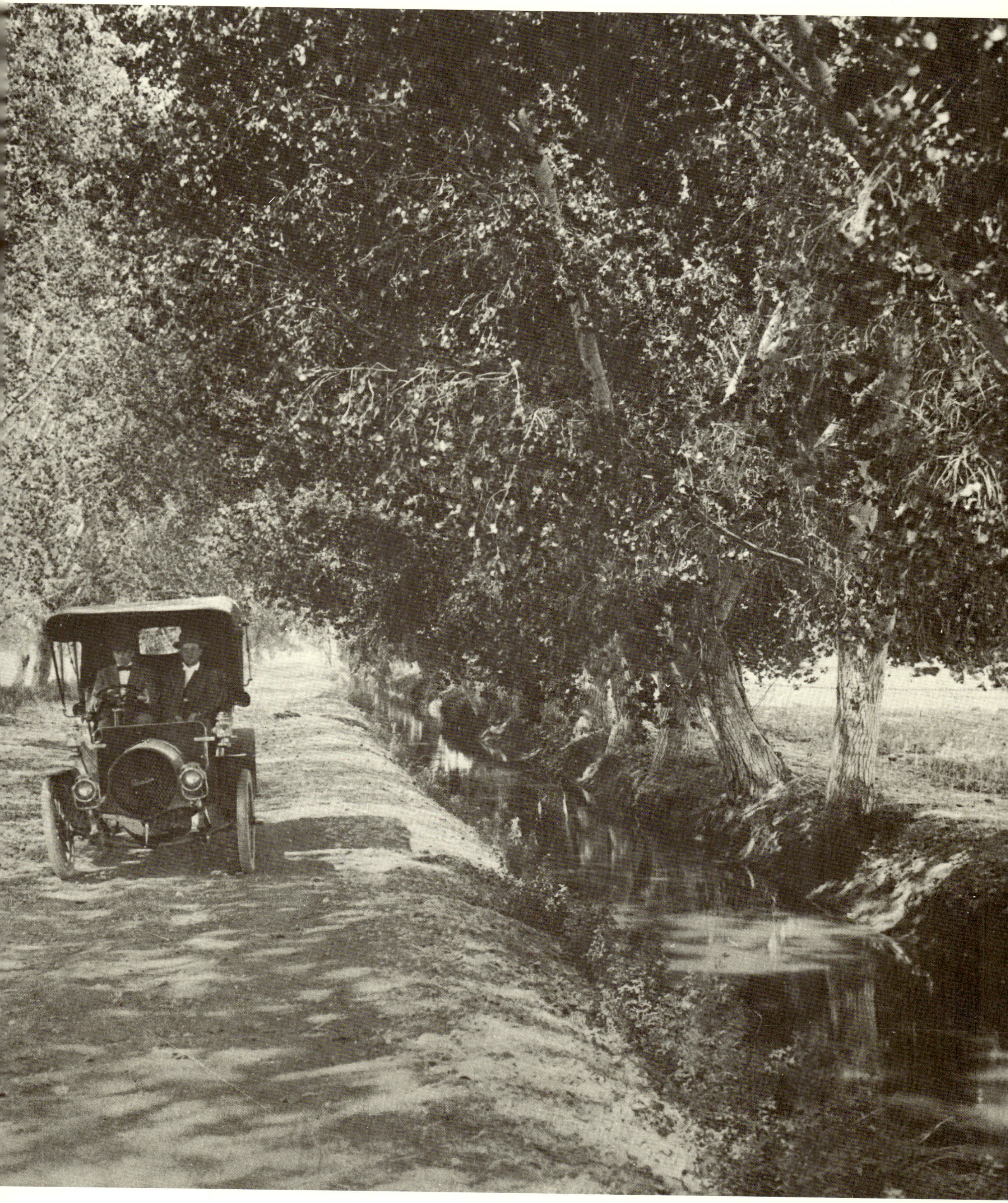

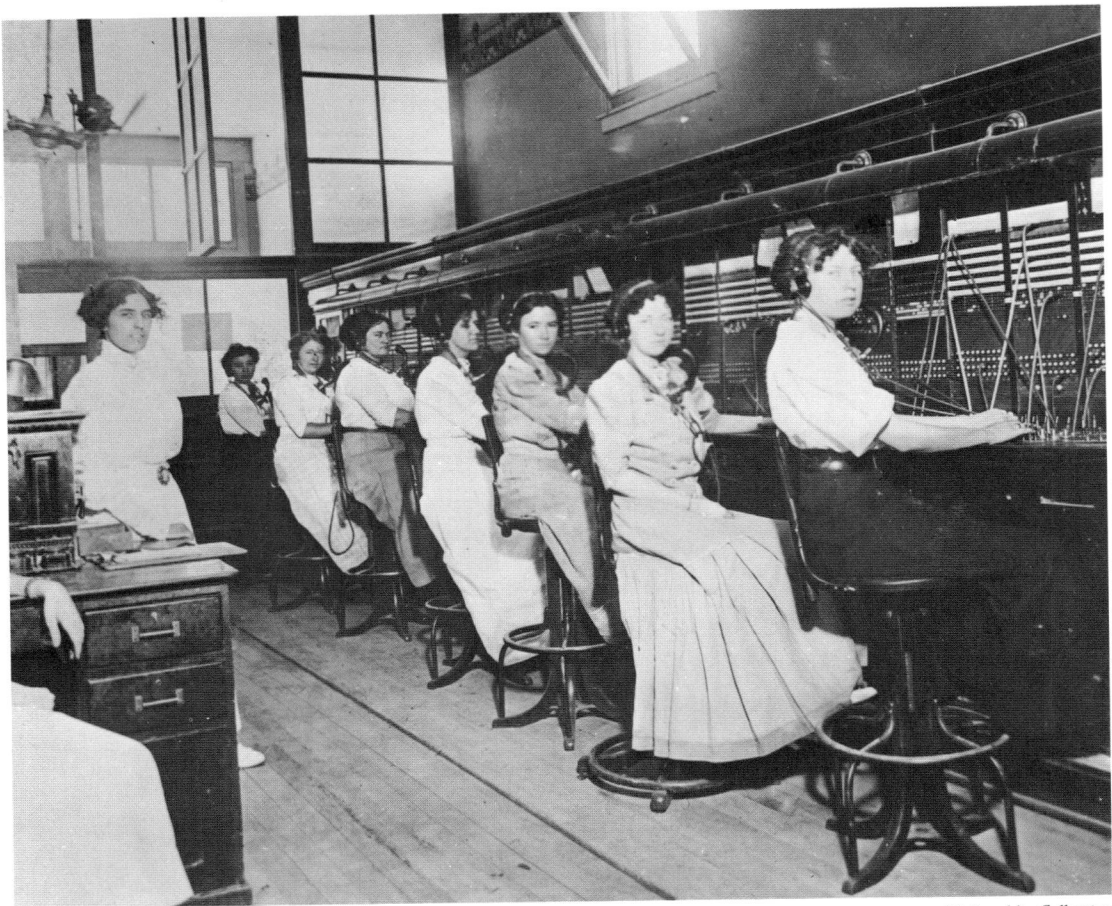

McLaughlin Collection

Cochise County Historical Society

106   Arizona Highways Album

University of Arizona Library

The isolation of territorial days was giving way to modern communication systems by 1910. (Upper left) Telephone operators at busy exchanges such as this one in Phoenix kept the conversations moving. (Lower left) In Douglas, delivery boys for the Douglas International *newspaper sped the latest news to subscribers. (Above) Wires hummed overhead in downtown Tucson. This scene at the corner of Congress and Stone shows the rows of telephone and telegraph poles.*

Arizona State Library

The Constitutional Convention of 1910

By John Goff

Arizona's constitution was born in a sixty-day convention session marked by prodigious work and frequent eruption of delegate tempers. Regarded at the time as one of the most radical of all the state charters, it was created in open defiance of stern warnings from President Taft.

The enabling act that put both New Mexico and Arizona on the final road to statehood had received final Congressional approval in mid-June of 1910 and was signed by President Taft on June 20. This was the long-awaited permission to hold a constitutional convention, the call of which was left to Governor Richard E. Sloan.

Although the territory had adopted the primary method of nominating candidates for office, the enabling act required that this be done in party conventions held at the county level. The Republicans and Democrats presented slates of those who aspired to be delegates, and the election was scheduled for September 12, 1910.

Organized labor, at that time stronger in Arizona than in almost any other part of the nation, considered running its own slate of candidates unless concessions were made to put into the constitution the provisions that labor wanted. These included the direct election of United States senators, an anti-injunction law, and the initiative, referendum, and recall. An agreement was made so that several of the Democrats became candidates with union support.

When results of the votes for fifty-two delegates were known, forty-one Democrats and eleven Republicans had been chosen. They gathered in the chamber of the House of Representatives on the third floor of the Arizona Capitol at noon on Monday, October 10, and were called to order by a Maricopa County delegate, Judge Albert C. Baker.

In their respective party caucuses, it had been decided that the Democrats would support for permanent president George W. P. Hunt of Globe and the Republicans would support Judge Edmund W. Wells of Prescott. Hunt was chosen by a straight party-line vote.

The Reverend Seaborn Crutchfield, a Methodist who had spent part of the Civil War in a Union prisoner of war camp, was chaplain, and his invocations were some of the most highly political praying ever heard. The Democrats were always in the right, in his eyes, and the Republicans somehow in league with the forces of evil.

A. W. Cole, not a delegate, was made permanent secretary of the convention, and other staff members were chosen. Several delegates felt there were too many employees, but Congress had appropriated $100,000 to hold the convention, and the majority view was that the money should be spent.

Among the delegates were a substantial number of able and prominent men. Three of them — Hunt, Dr. Benjamin B. Moeur, and Sidney P. Osborn — later held the governorship for more than a quarter-century. Mit

108 Arizona HIGHWAYS Album

...It is now proposed, at this very session of Congress, to pass the magic wand over the desert sands of Arizona and over the adobe huts of the humble Spanish-speaking people of New Mexico...they will become full partners in that limited government at Washington which bought them for a song from Mexico, and which ought to have dignity and firmness enough to keep them in their proper place of tutelage for perhaps forty years to come.

—Excerpt from "Two More Undeveloped States" in *The American Review of Reviews*, 1910 (Vol. 3)

Meeting at noon on October 10, 1910, with the temperature hovering around the 100-degree mark, Arizona's constitutional convention began its historic session. (Facing page) By October 31, when this picture was taken, the conferees had the new state charter well under way. President George W. P. Hunt is in the chair. (Above) The machinery for creating a new state, writing a constitution, and electing officials had been set in motion when President Taft signed the enabling act on June 20 of that year. "The President's Name on Statehood Bill," proclaimed The Arizona Republican. *But not everybody believed Arizona and New Mexico were ready for statehood. The commentary quoted above, from the influential* American Review of Reviews, *summarized the opposition's viewpoint. (Left) J. O. Dunbar, prominent Arizona publisher (hatless, center), is greeted in Tucson after returning from a Washington lobbying trip.*

McLaughlin Collection

Arizona Highways Album

Simms and Judge Wells were nominated for that office. Judge Baker, Donnel L. Cunningham, and Alfred Franklin served on the state Supreme Court, while Jacob Weinberger was later a federal district judge in California.

Mulford Winsor, Morris Goldwater, Everett E. Ellinwood, Charles M. Roberts, and Fred T. Colter later played important roles in politics, while John P. Orme, Carlos C. Jacome, and Edward A. Tovrea were important in the economic development of the new state.

John Langdon, a Republican, was a master mechanic, and James E. Crutchfield, the chaplain's son, was a Methodist minister. Other trades and occupations represented included railroad engineer, plumber, saloonkeeper, farmer, rancher, and lawyer.

The convention used the committee system. Three groups were concerned with operations, while twenty-one worked on various parts of the constitution. The convention met each morning and afternoon, and sometimes in the evening as well. The work seemed to go slowly at first; committees were in no hurry to report back.

Members introduced "propositions," 150 of them, containing material they thought should go into the charter. Delegates had before them constitutions of all the states, and they did much borrowing. Not to be overlooked as a cause for the slow progress was the fact that the Territorial Fair was in progress, and some delegates spent considerable time there.

Now and then tempers flared. When it was suggested that the delegation adjourn to go hear a speaker, Dr. Moeur retorted, "I think it would be of great benefit to Arizona if we get through with this constitution and let the doctor lecture next year." One day Donnel Cunningham of Cochise had been in a bad humor. The Copper Queen Band was visiting Phoenix, and a recess was taken to listen to it. Afterward the gentleman admitted that the music indeed had soothed a savage beast like him.

One morning Orrin Standage of Maricopa arose and explained that he knew his absence had been much "deplored and censured," but he hoped the box of cigars he was passing about would atone. "I hope you will enjoy them as much as I did my absence from the convention last night," he declared.

By early December, the constitution was in rough draft and ready to be considered, article by article, by the committee of the whole. Although President Hunt presided over the convention, others took turns chairing the committee of the whole. Michael G. Cunniff of Yavapai, a former Harvard English instructor, had the important task of providing the final wording of the constitution.

Although the delegates had been warned that President Taft would not accept the constitution if it contained a provision for the recall of judges, nevertheless such a feature was adopted.

The final meeting was held December 9, 1910. Only one Republican, John Langdon, signed the finished constitution; one Democrat, Everett E. Ellinwood, refused to sign. The others finally agreed to what was at the time considered a radical document. It was not really so, and such provisions as the decentralized executive system which it created were actually old-fashioned.

Hunt announced that the gavel used to preside over the meeting had disappeared, and no one would receive a final paycheck until it was returned. It mysteriously reappeared and is now on display in the Capitol.

An election was held February 9, 1911, at which time the voters were asked to approve or disapprove the constitution. There was a notable closing of ranks, and even Governor Sloan supported the proposed charter so that statehood could be achieved. Needed changes could be made later, he said. The voters, 12,584 to 3920, overwhelmingly approved what the convention had produced.

Then it was time for everyone to sit back and wait for what the Congress and the President would do.

JOHN S. GOFF, a lawyer as well as a historian, heads the Social Studies area at Phoenix College. His biography of Governor George W. P. Hunt and his writings on the Arizona constitutional convention and territorial government have earned him fame as a scholar and chronicler of Arizona history.

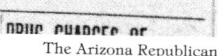

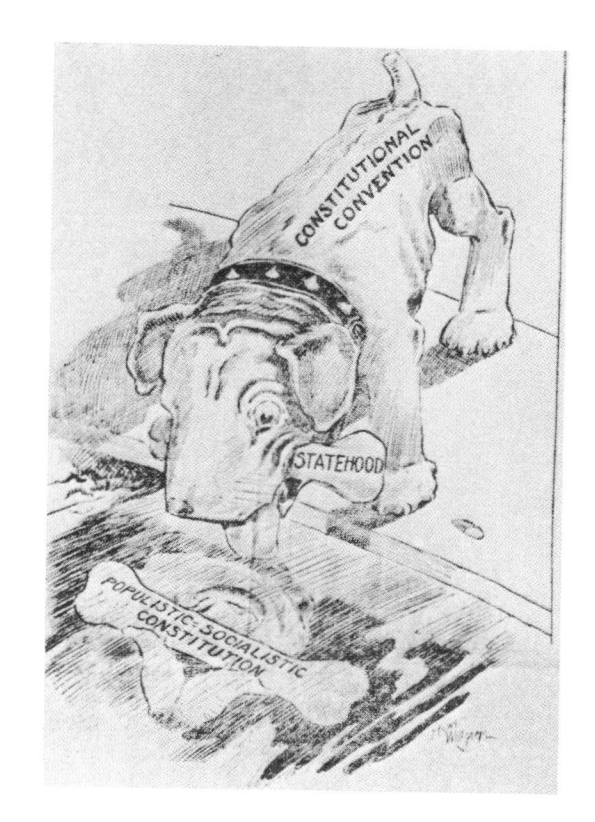

Members of the constitutional convention and their staff (facing page) left their duties at the capitol to pose for this often-reprinted photograph. (Top left) Four days away from adjournment of the convention, a Phoenix political cartoonist penned this view of the debate. That's A.C. Baker (speaking, at left), of Maricopa County, in the dark suit. (Top right) The Arizona Republican expressed editorial worry that the constitutional convention might drop the juicy bone of statehood, like the dog in the cartoon, for the illusion of a radical constitution. (Above) The election of state officers in December, 1911, would soon put these people out of work, but the last officials of Arizona Territory seemed content. Governor Richard Sloan is seated fourth from left.

Arizona Highways Album 111

McLaughlin Collection

McLaughlin Collection

National Archives

Desert Caballeros Museum

National Archives

It was no secret that much of the legislation that governed early twentieth-century Arizona was written and debated in the old Adams Hotel at Center Street and Adams in Phoenix (facing page). But the grand hostelry went up in flames in 1910. Towns all over the territory took pride in their hotels. (Top) Salome, on the dusty road to California, hosted tourists, as did the mountain town of Poland in Yavapai County (center). When Jerome was approaching its peak, visitors stayed at the Montana Hotel (above).

Arizona Highways Album   113

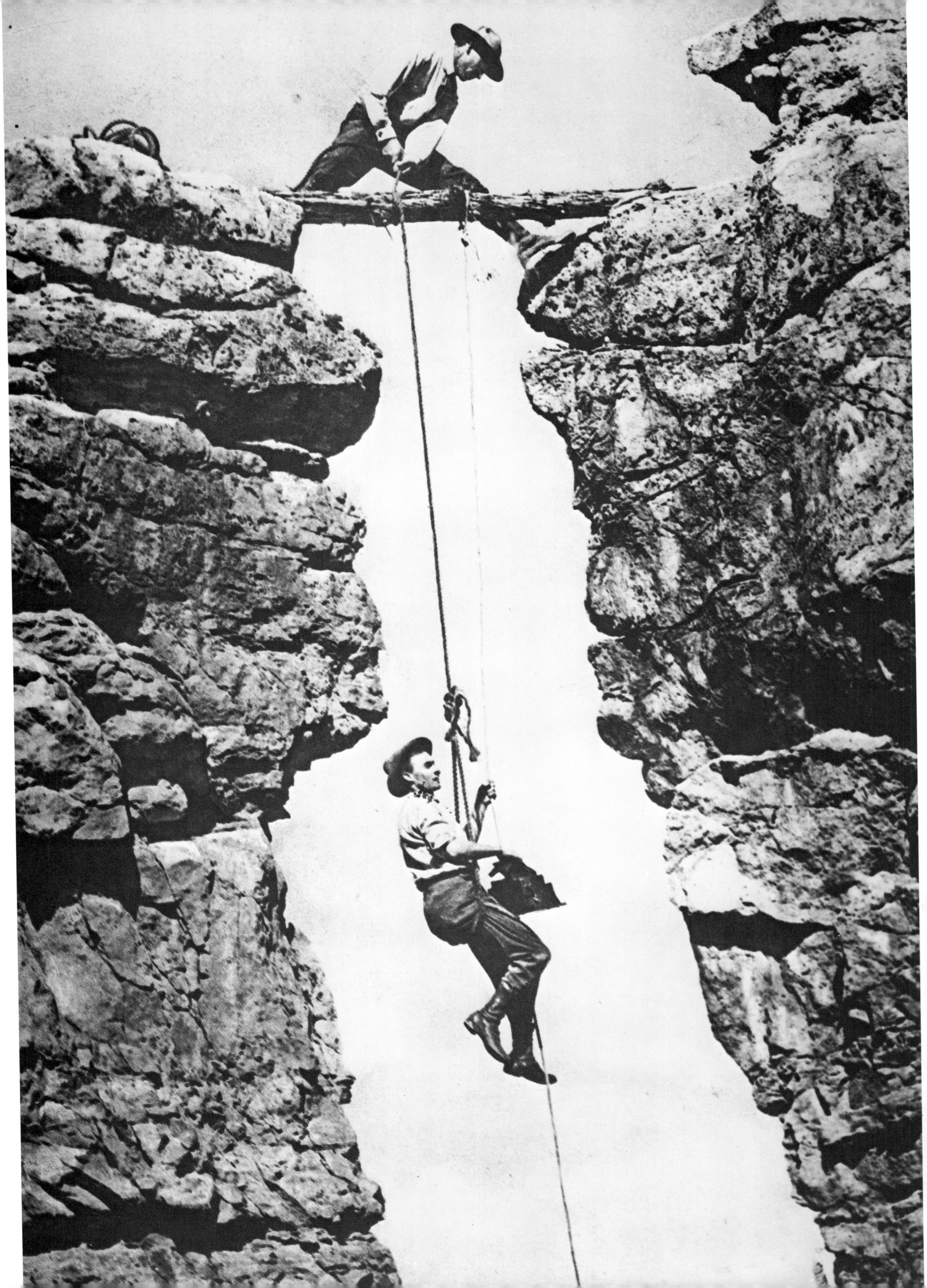

Northern Arizona University Library

Desert Caballeros Museum

Oh, the vexing problems of territorial life! In the long-lost days before hydraulic cranes, computerized gadgets, and jet air travel, Arizonans made do with whatever was on hand. (Facing page) Emery Kolb built much of his fame as a photographer of the Grand Canyon on his ability to shoot from unusual vantage points. He risked his life on the doubtful strength of a log and a helper's muscle. (Above) When the horse ran away, you had to get out and push the buggy. (Left) Eating watermelon, without utensils, in a white party dress was a challenge to ladies of the period.

McLaughlin Collection

Arizona Highways Album   115

Theodore Roosevelt Dam

By Earl Zarbin

Theodore Roosevelt Dam, sixty-five miles northeast of Phoenix, more than any other man-made structure symbolizes Arizona's statehood, progress, and prosperity.

With so many other wonders visible today, from Phoenix skyscrapers to aqueducts carrying water hundreds of miles across the desert, it may be difficult to understand Roosevelt Dam's importance to the framers of statehood.

For many years, residents of Arizona's central agricultural region, the Salt River Valley, had struggled to get a water storage dam on the Salt River in the Tonto Basin.

They knew that a dam would provide them with another powerful argument for statehood. The water held in storage would flow when needed, assuring life for their farmlands and generating new wealth, which would draw settlers and new investment. They knew population and wealth mattered in Washington, D.C., where statehood would be decided.

Most delegates to Arizona's constitutional convention in the fall of 1910 agreed. They saw in Roosevelt Dam's construction, which was almost completed by then, the demarcation between old and new, frontier and development, territory and state.

For that reason, the delegates featured the likeness of Roosevelt Dam and its reservoir in the Great Seal of the coming state. Spread before the dam were irrigated fields, orchards, and grazing cattle. The delegates did not ignore Arizona's other major industry, mining, but water storage and farming dominated.

When Roosevelt Dam was built, it was — and it remains today — the largest masonry arch dam in the world. From the deepest bedrock, it rises 284 feet. It is made of native stone cut from canyon walls where the spillways are located. When full, the reservoir holds 1,378,800 acre-feet of water.

The first official move toward building the dam came after the U. S. Senate in February, 1889, created a Select Committee on Irrigation and Reclamation of Arid Lands. The committee planned a Phoenix visit the following September.

In preparation for its arrival, the Maricopa County Board of Supervisors directed County Surveyor William Breckenridge to survey the Salt and Verde rivers northeast of Phoenix to find the most suitable site for the dam and reservoir.

Breckenridge and two

116   Arizona HIGHWAYS Album

Salt River Project

companions, including James H. McClintock, identified the Tonto Basin site, about 400 yards below where Tonto Creek drained into the Salt River, as the best.

"Surely," wrote McClintock, "the general government can find at no other place a more eligible site for water storage than this presents."

The Senate committee's visit produced no positive results, nor did formation of a private enterprise, the Hudson Reservoir and Canal Company, on February 18, 1893, despite a Phoenix newspaper's optimistic opinion that this was the beginning of "making a lake of Tonto Basin."

In 1897, Arthur Powell Davis, a U. S. Geological Survey engineer, visited Tonto Basin, and said, "It would probably be impossible to find anywhere in the arid region a storage project in which all conditions are as favorable as for this one."

Davis' enthusiasm did nothing to bring about construction. But later, when the Arizona legislature

Continued on page 120

Theodore Roosevelt, who had been succeeded in the Presidency by William Howard Taft two years before, made a triumphal visit to Arizona on March 18, 1911, to dedicate the giant dam named in his honor. (Far left) Flashing his famous grin, Roosevelt delivered his dedicatory address from a podium at the dam site. (Above) Completion of Roosevelt Dam near the confluence of the Salt River and Tonto Creek signaled the beginning of a great new era of irrigated agriculture in central Arizona and gave tremendous impetus to Arizona's bid for statehood. Members of the constitutional convention thought the dam so important that they featured it on the new Great Seal of Arizona.

Arizona Highways Album

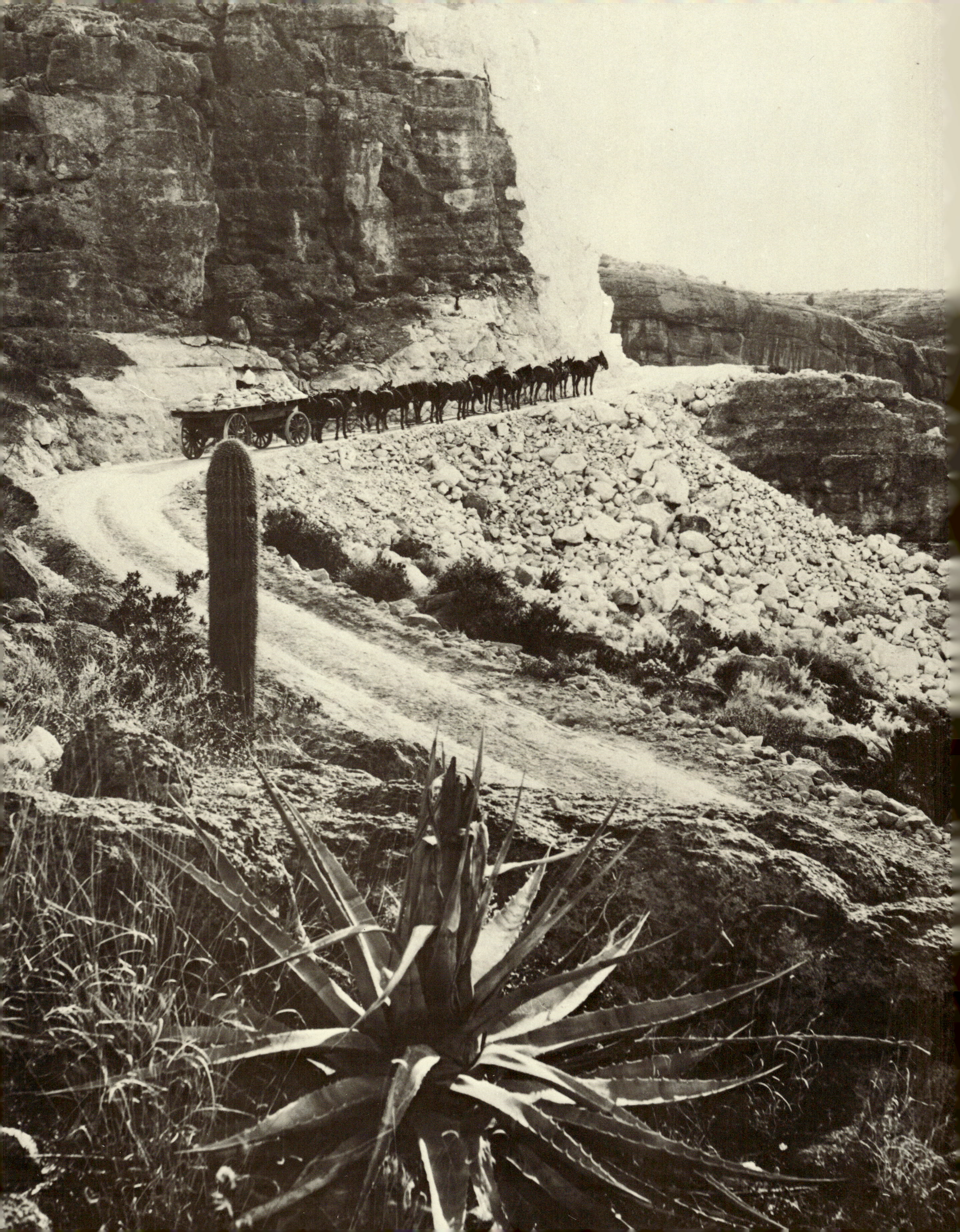

Salt River Project

McLaughlin Collection

(Facing page) Construction of Roosevelt Dam was one of the mightiest engineering feats of the early twentieth century. Before work could begin, a 63-mile road had to be built to transport materials and supplies to the almost inaccessible dam site. Teams of sixteen to twenty horses or mules were used to traverse the tortuous route—today's Apache Trail—between 1905 and 1911. (Above) Block by block, the masonry dam inched skyward. (Above right) Meanwhile, youthful zanjeros (irrigation workers) like these three still worked the old canals and awaited the new bonanza of water. (Right) Thieves stole water in those days, and vigilant ranchers used rifles to protect their water rights.

Salt River Project

Arizona Highways Album

Roosevelt attracted big crowds wherever he went in Arizona, where the citizens had forgiven Teddy's support of Arizona-New Mexico joint statehood. (Below) On returning from the dedication of Roosevelt Dam, he spoke from the steps of Old Main at Tempe Normal School. (Bottom) Wherever he went in the Southwest, he enjoyed reunions with his Rough Riders comrades. (Right) Roosevelt's touring car led a happy parade to and from the dam dedication.

Arizona State University Archives

McLaughlin Collection

Continued from page 117

passed a law allowing Maricopa County to create a Board of Water Storage Commissioners to build reservoirs, Davis drew plans for the dam.

Before Maricopa County could act, however, federal lawmakers passed the National Reclamation Act. Proposed in December, 1901, by President Theodore Roosevelt, the law permitted federal aid in building dams. It was signed by Roosevelt on June 17, 1902, and Davis gave key support for the Tonto Basin dam as one of the first projects.

First, though, Salt River Valley

Salt River Project

farmers and ranchers had to organize to repay the government the cost of building the dam. Out of this need came the Salt River Valley Water Users' Association, which incorporated February 7, 1903, and is one of two organizations known jointly today as the Salt River Project.

Because money for Roosevelt Dam was to come from the national government, the Geological Survey engineers who created the U.S. Reclamation Service to build it were able to exploit more fully the dam's hydroelectric possibilities. Hence, water storage and generation of electricity represent the twin faces of reclamation.

After the dam was approved for construction, the engineers decided to build a road — today's Apache Trail — between Mesa and the dam site. The sixty-three-mile road cost $350,644 and opened April 24, 1905, becoming the route for men, equipment, and supplies.

The dam's cornerstone was laid September 20, 1906, even while excavation for the dam continued.

Long before Theodore Roosevelt dedicated the dam on March 18, 1911, it began storing water and producing the electricity that helped make Maricopa County the region's most populous and fulfilled the visions of those who thought the dam would abet the drive for statehood.

EARL ZARBIN, a longtime newspaper reporter and history buff, has devoted much time in recent years to researching and writing about the Roosevelt Dam and the Salt River. He has published two books about central Arizona's great reclamation project and plans others relating to Arizona water history.

Arizona Highways Album 121

ODE TO BILLY TAFT

(Published in the Florence Blade-Tribune, *November, 1911)*

We will tolerate your gall
And surrender our recall
Till safe within the statehood stall,
Billy Taft, Billy Taft.

Then we'll fairly drive you daft
With the ring of our horse laugh,
Billy Taft, Billy Taft.

As we joyously re-install
By the vote of one and all,
That ever-glorious recall
Billy Taft, Billy Taft!

— Colonel Thomas Weedin

Mr. Taft Says 'No'
Continued from page 102

Those Arizonans, Democrats and Republicans alike, relayed Taft's warning. *The Arizona Republican* of Phoenix fretted over it in frequent editorials and ran a cartoon showing a foolish dog (Arizona) dropping the bone of statehood so it could grab at a watery reflection labeled "populistic, socialistic constitution."

All Arizona, and much of Washington, waited breathlessly for the decision, as the people chose their delegates to the constitutional convention. Would they elect safe, solid Republicans such as Carlos Jacome of Tucson, or at least moderate Democrats like Morris Goldwater of Prescott? Or would they choose such radicals as Democrat George W. P. Hunt of Globe, who was backed by the powerful labor unions?

The September, 1910, election results surprised everyone, elating the Hunt crowd and throwing the business-oriented Republicans into a panic. Of the fifty-two delegates chosen, only eleven were Republicans. The Democratic "progressives" were in the saddle, and they would certainly adopt the most radical kind of constitution.

Mournfully, the *Republican* observed that statehood, so recently a sure thing, was now only a remote possibility.

What kind of Arizona was this territory panting for statehood in 1910? Where did her people live, and what manner of work did they do?

For modern-day Arizonans, it may come as a shock to learn that the most populous county of the territory at the time of the constitutional convention was not Maricopa, where well over half of Arizona's people live today, nor Pima, nor Yavapai. The county with the largest population, and therefore the most delegates, was Cochise, in the territory's far southeast corner. Legendary Tombstone was past its peak in 1910, and only one Cochise delegate was elected from the town. The major communities were Bisbee and Douglas, whose mines and smelters poured forth their coppery abundance around the clock. Each city sent three delegates, and the Bisbee suburb of Lowell sent another.

The ten Cochise delegates were joined by nine from agricultural Maricopa County; six from Yavapai; five each from Gila, Graham, and Pima; and twelve others scattered among seven other counties. Greenlee County had just been created and was not yet eligible to send representatives.

Many of the prominent families of Arizona were represented at the convention — Orme, Tovrea, Goldwater, Ellinwood, and others. It is difficult to understand how such a distinguished assemblage could have been considered "wildly radical" by a large segment of the press. Once in session, they proved themselves to be sober, hard-working, and capable.

The constitution they produced in mid-December of 1910 was as progressive as the conservatives feared

President Taft said "No" in no uncertain terms when Arizona's constitutional convention defied him and included judicial recall in its charter. (Above) Florence publisher Thomas Weedin, pictured early in his career, penned this ditty expressing Arizona's contempt for Taft's veto threat. (Facing page) No cartoon of this era of Arizona birth pangs could more graphically portray Taft's determination to keep Arizona out of the Union until it agreed to eliminate recall of judges from its constitution.

(only one Republican delegate was willing to sign it). It contained the initiative, the referendum, and Taft's hated provision for recalling elected officials.

The distraught Governor Sloan declared that Arizona's chances for statehood under this constitution were "about the same as for annexation to the Russian empire."

But the people loved it, and they showed their overwhelming approval at the polls in 1911. Now the decision was in the hands of Congress and President Taft. Like bad little boys caught with their fingers in the cookie jar, the people of Arizona awaited their spanking from the portly President.

It came as promised, with Taft sending the constitution back for deletion of the offending recall provision. Much as they hungered for recall, Arizonans longed even more passionately for statehood. They went back to the polls and approved the constitution without recall.

No dummies they, Arizona voters knew full well they could reinstate the controversial provision as soon as they had joined the Union. Taft knew it, too, but he felt he had done his duty.

Sure enough, the recall provision was put back into the constitution as one of the first orders of business by the new State of Arizona.

Arizona Highways Album

Chapter V
And The Bells Rang Out

President William Howard Taft had delayed Arizona's entry into statehood until the territory's voters agreed to eliminate judicial recall from their new constitution. In February, 1912, all was in readiness for Arizona's big day, but Taft delayed it twice more: first, because February 12 was Lincoln's Birthday, a federal holiday; and second, because he considered February 13 unlucky. But on the morning of Wednesday, February 14, he affixed his signature to the Arizona statehood proclamation. Ralph Cameron, Arizona's delegate to Congress, is shown directly above the President's pen.

THE ARIZONA REPUBLICAN

THE WEATHER: Arizona — Fair Tuesday and Wednesday; Not Much Change in Temperature.

THE REPUBLICAN: Fair, Candid, Straightforward—A newspaper for all the people.

TWENTY-SECOND YEAR — 12 PAGES — PHOENIX, ARIZONA, WEDNESDAY MORNING, FEBRUARY 14, 1912. — 12 PAGES — VOL. XXII. NO. 269.

The Forty-eighth State Steps Into the Union Today

PORTALS SWING WIDE TO ADMIT THE NEW STATE
President Will Sign Proclamation and Arizona Will Step Into Union at Eight O'clock Today Mountain Time.

PLANS COMPLETE FOR BIG EVENT
Inaugural Ceremonies Will be of the Simplest Character But the After Exercises Will be Most Hilarious.

NO LUXURIOUS BENZINE BUGGY FOR GOV. HUNT
Will Walk to the Capitol and Thus Set an Example of Thrift for Everybody.

SAYS HE COULD AFFORD TO RIDE
But Mr. Hunt Fears if He Did So He Might Lead Some of the Rest of us Astray.

¶ Hon. George W. P. Hunt, who today becomes first governor of the state of Arizona. Mr. Hunt is a business man of Globe, where he is heavily interested in a mercantile enterprise. He was also president of the constitutional convention and is an advocate of insurgent doctrines ▫ ▫ ▫ ▫

ARIZONA WILL DON THE GARB OF STATEHOOD
Glorious Climax of Long Fight Will Come With Signing of Proclamation Today.

HISTORY IS A SPLENDID ONE
Population is Small But it Possesses the Spirit That Has Made the West.

LOOKS FORWARD TO BECOMING A STYLISH ANGEL
Hill Files Plans and Specifications for His Choice in Matter of Feathers.

RED AND WHITE WILL SUIT HIM
Some Rather Picturesque Testimony is Given by Him Before House Committee.

Valentine's Day, 1912...the day Arizona's dreams came true...the emancipation from nearly half a century of territorial bondage.

In the year leading to the celebration, events moved rapidly for the territory. First, Arizona voters in February, 1911, approved the new constitution. Then Congress accepted the constitution and sent it to the White House.

As he had vowed to do, President Taft vetoed it on August 15, with a stinging comment that judicial recall was "so destructive of the independence of the judiciary...and so injurious to the cause of free government that I must disapprove the constitution containing it." But a week later, Taft signed a joint Congressional resolution calling for the entry of both New Mexico and Arizona, if the people of Arizona would remove the offending provision.

This the people did. In the general election of December 12, 1911, they voted in the slate of officials who will forever be revered as the first to serve the State of Arizona.

Seldom had politicking been so emotional and so much in earnest as in that campaign of autumn, 1911.

Many of the big names of Arizona history were involved in that battle for political immortality: Marcus Smith, Ralph Cameron, and Henry Fountain Ashurst, each yearning to be one of Arizona's first U. S. senators; Carl Hayden, the Maricopa County sheriff who aspired to serve in the House of Representatives; George W. P. Hunt, the odds-on favorite for governor; and Sidney P. Osborn, the callow youth who was asking the people to make him the first secretary of state.

The Senate race was of particular national interest. Here was brash, unpolished Arizona preparing to send two unknowns to the Senate chamber that once echoed to the oratory of Clay, Webster, and Calhoun. Republican Cameron, Arizona's territorial delegate to Congress, and his Democratic predecessor, Marcus Smith, were the best known. In that Democratic year, the winners were Smith and his running mate, Ashurst. Arizona's single seat in the House went to the popular Carl Hayden, whose Democratic ties helped to make him the easy winner over Republican J. S. Williams. Hayden, who declared, "I'm a workhorse, not a showhorse," was to serve in Congress—first the House, later the Senate—for fifty-seven years.

In state races, observers paid special attention to Osborn, whose election as secretary of state made him the youngest man (twenty-eight) ever chosen for that high post in any state. Osborn later would be one of Arizona's most able governors.

The governor's race was fought more bitterly in the partisan press than on the hustings. It was really decided in the October primary, when Hunt bested Florence publisher Thomas Weedin. The Republicans ran elderly Judge Edmund Wells of Prescott. Hunt

Continued on page 144

Statehood at last! As the last hours of territorial status ticked away (facing page), Arizona's newspapers headlined the biggest story of this or any day. (Above) Bands, cadets, dignitaries—all marched in the February 14 Statehood Day parade down Washington Street in Phoenix. (Right) Two men destined for fame on Washington's Capitol Hill were Senator Henry Fountain Ashurst, left, and Representative Carl Hayden.

COOK WITH GAS

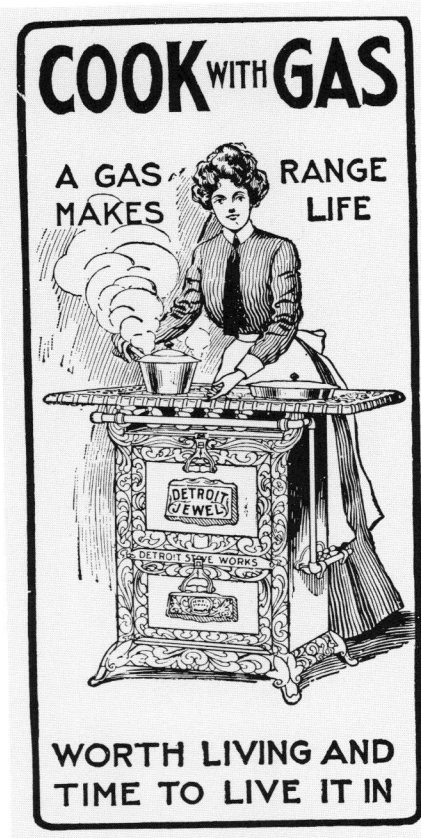

A GAS RANGE MAKES LIFE

WORTH LIVING AND TIME TO LIVE IT IN

Pacific Gas AND Electric Co.
PHOENIX, ARIZONA

M. Goldwater & Bro.
"THE BEST ALWAYS"

Better Corsets

That's the secret of better fitting gowns. Well dressed women probably pay more attention to their corset than any other garment. On it primarily depends the smartness of their appearance.

Thompson's Glove Fitting CORSETS.

Are better corsets, superior in style and fit, superior in quality. **Made in many models and lengths to fit every figure.**

NEW MODELS $1 to $5.

THOMSON'S "GLOVE-FITTING" CORSETS

A MODEL FOR EVERY FIGURE

Dress Skirts
Our Regular $9.00 and $10 Line of Dress Skirts—All at one price, at a great saving. Built of A-1 quality Worsted materials in solid colors and novelty effects, full pleated skirts; Tunic style predominating — special for Monday $6.98

Tub Suits
Two and Three-Piece Suits, also a sample line of Linen Dresses, exclusive styles, superbly trimmed, white and colors, quite an enticing aggregation of models; formerly sold up to $30—for Monday, choice..............$9.98

$1.98
for pick of 47 dozen high-class

Lingerie Waists
Our banner $3.00 and $3.50 collection, several styles, each and every one the very acme of beauty, trimmed in filet Lace, Val. lace and Baby Irish. No trading stamps with these.

$4.29
for choice of complete stock of $6.00

Wash Suits and Dresses
Made of various representative tub materials, such as poplin, French linen, rep, zephyr and pure linen.

$7.45
for the Free Choice of All Our $10.00 and $12.50

Linen Suits
Long Coat tailored models, made of homespun crash, in lavender, reseda, white, natural, old rose and Copenhagen; have collar and cuffs trimmed in black poplin.

All Our $2.50 and $3.00 Street Dresses
A choice lot, made of plain and fancy wash materials; high neck and Dutch neck effects—for Monday only, choice

$1.98

$22.50, $25.00, $27.50, $30.00 Silk Dresses
A large lot of them, latest Tunic and Peasant styles, made of either Taffeta, Pongee or Foulard, in a choice collection of colorings and patterns—for Monday only, choice

$14.98

Children's Dresses
Our Regular $2.50 Line— For misses as well, Co-Ed and Russian Blouse models galore, made of Zephyr Gingham and Percale in solid colors and fancy designs—for Monday, choice....$1.89

½ Price
for all our
Tailored Cloth Suits

Kimonos
A Considerable Lot of **Women's Short Kimonos** —Made of prettily figured Lawn, mostly light patterns, cheap at 25c— for Monday, without trading stamps, at......14c

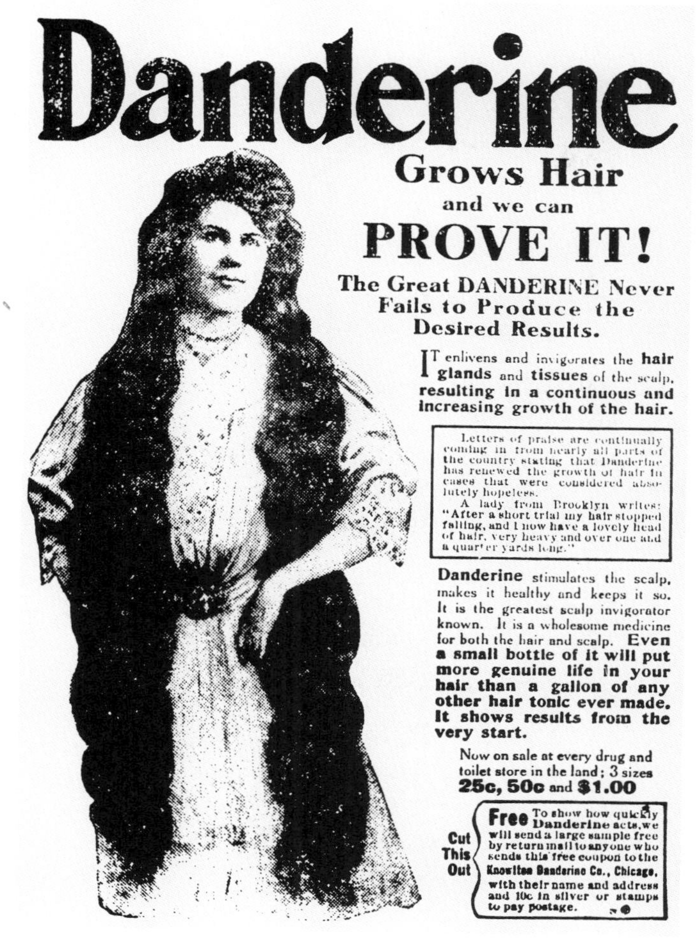

Advertisements in Arizona's daily newspapers on Statehood Day (courtesy of the Arizona Historical Foundation) mirrored the lives of Arizona's people in 1912. (Facing page, lower left) Milady could buy a dress for as little as $1.98. (Upper left) After a lifetime of wood stoves, gas ranges meant sheer heaven. (Upper right) Wasp waists required heavy-duty corsets. (Above, upper left) A lady's hair deserved the best. (Upper right) People flocked to buy the amazing new player pianos. (Lower left) Newspaper subscription contests offered big prizes. (Lower right) Male vanity was running strong in 1912.

Arizona Highways Album 129

Men Who Made The State

By C. L. Sonnichsen

Statehood was the Promised Land for the Territory of Arizona for twenty-three years, from 1889 to 1912. Territorial Governor Meyer Zulick sounded the first trumpet in 1888 when he told the legislature that the time had come to end Arizona's "tutelage." The next year, the assault on Washington began.

Statehood was a bipartisan matter. Republicans and Democrats who despised each other personally and politically joined forces on this one great issue. Everybody contributed—merchants and miners, lumbermen and lawyers, editors and engineers—but the standard-bearers were men with clout in Washington: governors and delegates in Congress.

Of those whose names might be mentioned, half a dozen stand out. They were all battle-scarred veterans of the political wars, and some of them had feet of almost pure clay, but they were all on the side of the angels in one respect: they believed that every man in Arizona (some wanted to include women) should be able to vote for President—that Arizona should be a state.

Delegate to Congress Marcus Aurelius Smith, a Tombstone lawyer with roots in Indiana, opened the campaign in 1889 and stayed on the firing line until he was defeated—for the first time—in 1908. His appearance was deceptive. Small, thin, and never robust physically, he presented to the world in later years a face that reminded one of a friendly bloodhound, with sad eyes and drooping jowls, but he was a personal and political powerhouse; so successful in being all things to all voters, he was known (in Republican circles) as Marcus Octopus Smith. A dedicated Democrat, he had so many supporters in both parties that he long seemed unbeatable at the polls.

As a territorial delegate, Smith had no vote in Congress, but he had the floor, and he used it brilliantly. In 1889 he mesmerized the House into approving statehood, but the Senate refused to go along. The Republican solons wanted no more Democratic senators, and they were afraid of "free silver," accepted as gospel by Arizona and Delegate Smith, which would have placed silver on a par with gold as legal tender.

Smith realized that territories aspiring to statehood needed to support each other, and, in 1902, he joined forces with the delegates from Oklahoma and New Mexico to introduce an omnibus bill that would have authorized enabling legislation for all three.

Supporting him in this campaign was another popular and powerful standard-bearer, two-time Arizona Governor (1892, 1898-1902) Nathan Oakes Murphy, a native of Maine who became a resident of Prescott in 1883. Politics appealed to him more than business, and he rose rapidly to power and prestige. His second term was marred by personal and financial scandals, but he stood shoulder to shoulder with Smith on the omnibus bill. His prestige as governor helped it to pass the House, but it encountered massive resistance in the Senate.

In that year of 1902, while the fate of the bill was in the balance, Smith and Murphy drew unwilling and unforeseen support from the foremost opponent of statehood—Senator Albert J. Beveridge of Indiana, chairman of the powerful Committee on Territories. Starting as a country lawyer, he had risen to the top in Washington and was admired nationally as a man of the highest principles, a speaker of power and authority (he wrote a textbook on the art of oratory), a believer in the virtues of the Common Man.

Beveridge admired Abraham Lincoln who, like himself, was "a man of the people and of the soil," but his common men, unfortunately for Arizona and New Mexico, were white Anglo-Saxon Protestants. Mexicans and Indians were unlettered, probably could not speak English, and would be poor risks as citizens. Oklahoma was possibly "American" enough to pass muster; Arizona and New Mexico were suspect.

To prepare for the vote on the omnibus bill, scheduled for December, 1902, Beveridge led a

Ralph H. Cameron

Nathan O. Murphy

Joseph H. Kibbey

subcommittee on a whirlwind tour of the three territories, arriving at Phoenix on November 17. He spent three days in Arizona, moving so fast that Mark Smith commented acidly, "I met the committee—I never could have overtaken it." In Smith's opinion, Beveridge was looking for ignorance, corruption, and sin in Arizona and found what he was seeking. *The Arizona Republican* declared hopefully that Beveridge had found "a high degree of civilization" in Phoenix and Tucson and Bisbee and that the report would be favorable, but that proved to be wishful thinking. Beveridge said no. Arizona was too sparsely populated, too illiterate, too lawless to be ready for statehood. Arizonans were furious.

Without intending to, Beveridge had given new impetus to the quest for statehood. Almost immediately he made the issue still more emotional by suggesting that, since there were too few people in either Arizona or New Mexico to make a state, the two territories should be admitted to the Union as one. Arizona disapproved violently. Smith commented that Beveridge had rejected one rotten egg but thought that two rotten eggs would make a good omelet.

In January, 1903, the original omnibus bill came up for a vote. Beveridge killed it by staying away from the capitol for a week, knowing that no action would be taken in the absence of the chairman of the Committee on Territories.

The question of "jointure" for Arizona and New Mexico was still very much alive, however, and it brought a fourth standard-bearer to the front lines. Former Arizona Supreme Court Justice Joseph H. Kibbey took office as Arizona governor in 1905 by appointment of President Roosevelt. This just and gentlemanly immigrant from Indiana had won applause for his handling of the touchy issue of water rights, and no evil had been spoken of him until he came out against jointure, defying what amounted to orders from the President. Accused loudly of disloyalty, he nevertheless stuck to his guns and proposed to let the people decide. If the voters of either territory proved unwilling, jointure would be dead.

The idea caught on in Washington, and a new delegation of lawmakers came to Arizona to see if Beveridge had been right. This time the substantial men of the area took no chances. A special train of six private cars was waiting for the visitors, furnished with everything to make glad the heart of a congressman, and Arizona's Smith added a final flourish by taking them to the Grand Canyon. They went away persuaded that Beveridge had been wrong.

The Arizona and New Mexico territories voted on jointure in November, 1906. New Mexico favored it, but Arizona declared against the scheme almost six to one.

In fairness, Mark Smith should have been in at the finish of the Arizona statehood battle, but he was defeated in 1908 in a Republican landslide. In his last speech before the House he said sadly, "From early manhood my life has been dedicated to this holy cause, and I find myself now in poverty with hair as white as the snows on her mountain tops, still pleading the cause of Arizona."

As the new congressional delegate, Ralph Cameron took up where Smith left off. In January, 1910, he made a fine speech calling for statehood, and President Taft signed the enabling act on June 20. Less than a week later, Governor Richard E. Sloan issued a call for delegates to the constitutional convention. The long war was over when George W. P. Hunt, in massive majesty, took office as governor of the forty-eighth state. Mark Smith went off to Washington again, this time as a senator and this time with a vote.

C. L. SONNICHSEN of Tucson has become a legend in the field of Southwest history. For many years a professor of English at what is now the University of Texas at El Paso, he has written many highly successful books and scores of articles on the history of the Southwest.

Arizona Highways Album

Senator Albert Beveridge and some other Congressional visitors found Arizona too sparsely populated and undeveloped for statehood. But those who knew the people best were sure that Arizonans were ready for the big step. (Top) Some settlements, like the one at Gold Road Mine in Mohave County, were small, but the people dressed like New Yorkers. (Above) The good, hardworking folk of the Buckeye area kept up with current events at the post office. (Right) And where could you find more adorable children than these Phoenix tots, ready for a party?

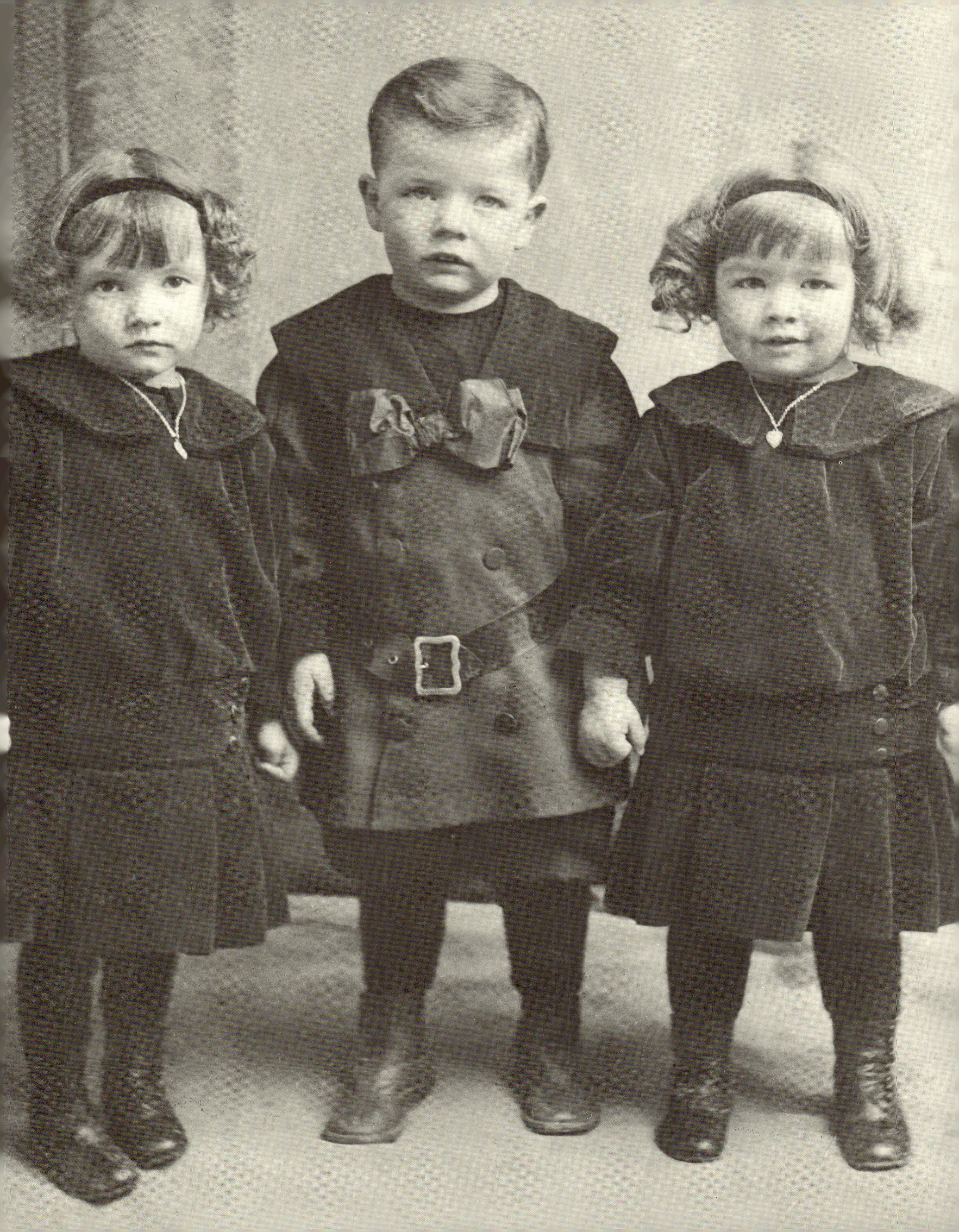

Arizona Highways Album

Arizona Historical Society, Tucson

Arizona Historical Foundation

Arizona State Library

All over Arizona, during the last interminable months of territorial bondage, people waited for the good news of statehood. (Left) Visitors to the bigger cities, such as these guests at the Tucson Park View Hotel, kept abreast of progress toward the goal. (Top) Fun-loving Prescott folks decorated their cars for a parade. (Above) And at Loretto School in Bisbee, children prepared for patriotic exercises.

Arizona Highways Album 135

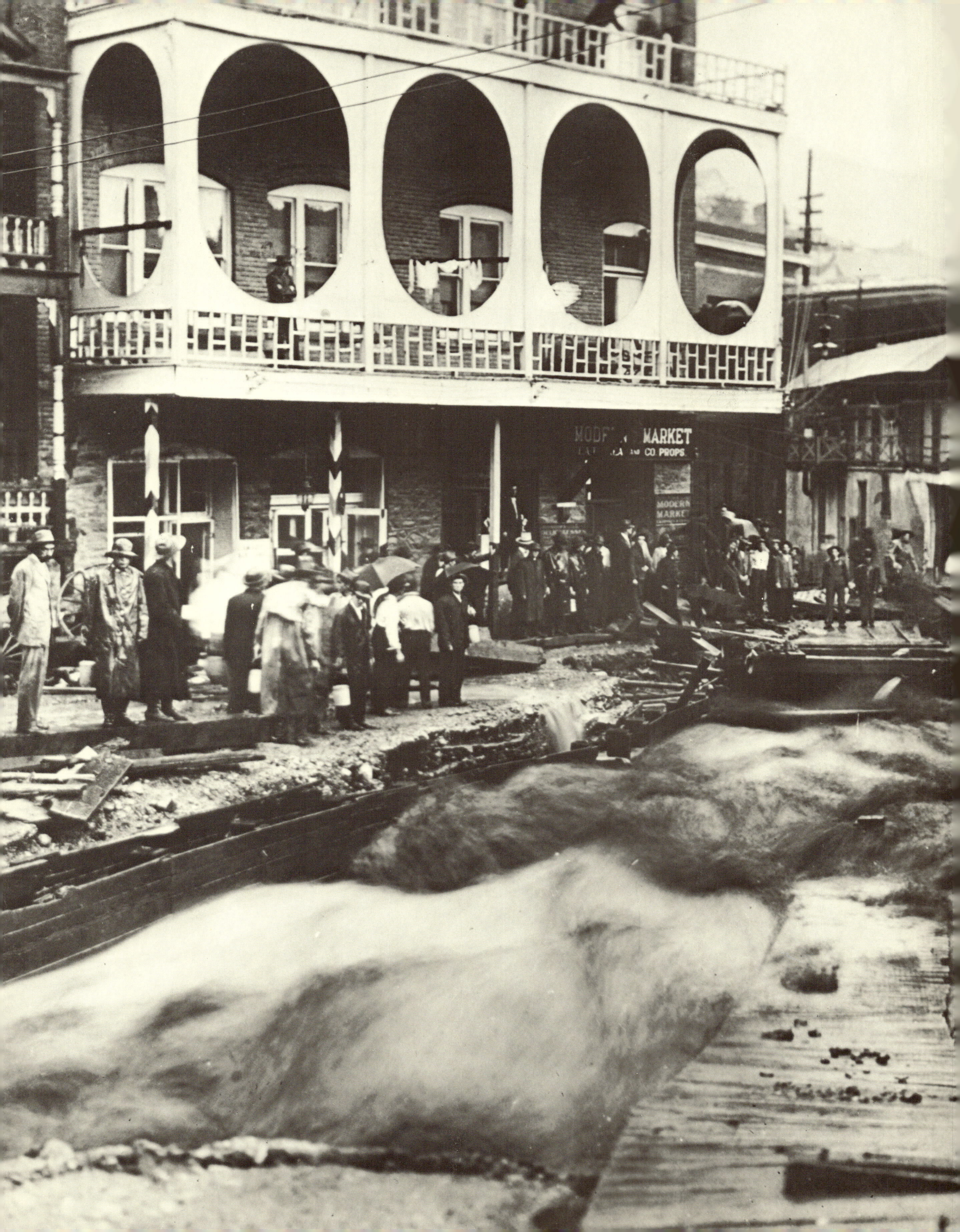
MARKET
CO PROPS.

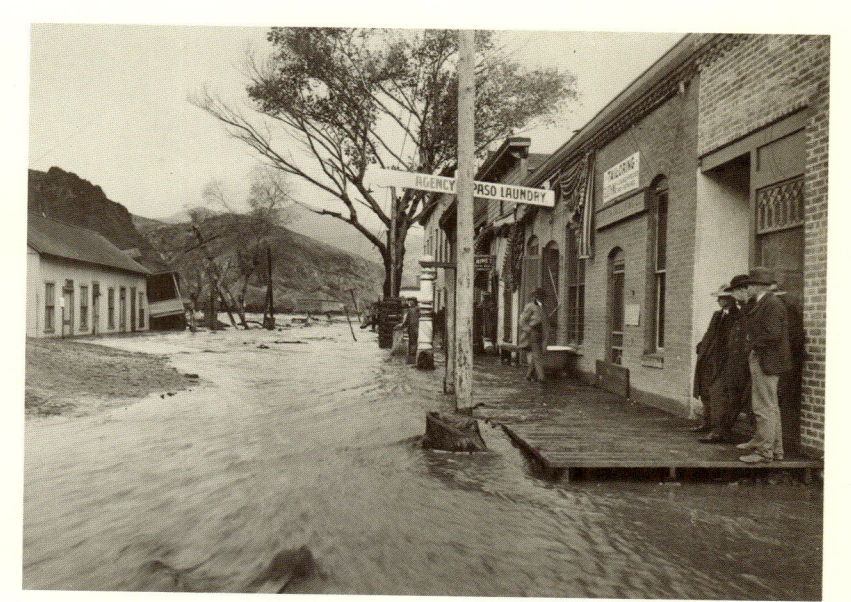

Among the many misconceptions about Arizona that persisted around the nation was that the territory was always bone-dry. Those who lost their homes, farms, and stores in the frequent floods knew otherwise. (Facing page) The disastrous flood of October, 1908, wreaked havoc in downtown Bisbee. (Top left) The Territorial Capitol in Phoenix was often marooned by floodwaters. (Top right) Clifton was frequently ravaged by the rampaging San Francisco River. (Above left) Downtown Glendale merchants knew all about flood damage. (Above right) So did members of the Phoenix Country Club on West Van Buren Street. Despite the many dams and flood control devices of today, Arizona still sometimes suffers such inundations.

Arizona Highways Album 137

Now, B'Gosh, Even the Grub Tastes Better

By Don Dedera

In the darkness of territorial obscurity, Arizona had been sprinting flat out for five decades. But when statehood finally came, it entered with a slow, sun-splashed, somewhat comic sashay.

For many a pioneer, it had been a long, bitter struggle. Two unexpected and unnecessary delays were added to the tension when President William Howard Taft out of petulance refused to admit Arizona on Lincoln's Birthday; then out of superstition withheld his signature on the thirteenth day of the month.

Now the day of fulfillment: February 14, 1912.

Awaiting the flash from Washington were a people made snappishly independent by federal abuse and neglect. They had not only endured Geronimo, confiscatory freight rates, and libelous journalism, but a Congress that had seriously proposed naming the territory "Gadsonia" after the Gadsden Purchase.

Rallying around the poetry of Sharlot Hall, they had noisily defeated joint statehood with New Mexico. And they had gambled the whole game by adopting the nation's most progressive constitution. This was the moment of a thousand victories.

At 10:23 A.M. Washington time on St. Valentine's Day, motion picture cameras whirred for the first time at an official Presidential ceremony. Abruptly, in Phoenix, a telegraph key clattered out the official message from the President:

"I have this morning signed the proclamation declaring Arizona to be a state...."

A stack of forty-eight sticks of dynamite echoed the people's approval in Bisbee. In Globe a cannon spoke forty-eight times. Engineers yanked whistle cords on boilers of locomotives, laundries, factories, mines, creameries, and mills.

In Tucson the siren at the waterworks wailed, while University of Arizona R.O.T.C. cadets crisply executed close-order drill. In Prescott, Whiskey Row raised a toast of firewater and pistol shots, and Arizona-born boys and girls tossed handfuls of earth to nurture a native white oak transplanted to the plaza. A parade marched around the Yavapai County Courthouse. In Flagstaff, a newsman wrote, "Now, b'gosh, even the grub tastes better."

Governor-elect George W. P. Hunt received the word in his quarters at the Ford Hotel in downtown Phoenix. Hunt was a picture politician of his day. Portly, bullet-headed, owlish behind circular lenses, magnificently mustachioed, he had almost mystic magnetism for the masses.

Now he turned to his speech writer and executive secretary, Mulford Winsor, and said, "Well, it is time to go."

Hunt had pleaded for modesty and restraint for his inaugural. But on Second Avenue, despite the governor's wishes, an impressive motorcade was forming for the journey to the state capitol on the western edge of the little town.

"I shall walk," he had announced, spurning half a dozen invitations to ride. Thus he projected his message to the pressing crowds that would elect him again and again: "My walk, may it be symbolic of the economies of my administration."

The entourage matched Hunt's snailish pace. Bands from the

Continued on page 143

Leonard Monti Collection

As Statehood Day dawned, all Arizona stood poised to celebrate the long-awaited event. Dynamite charges were prepared, cannons were loaded, and parades formed. (Facing page) The telegraph clattered out the news from Washington: "President Taft has signed the proclamation!" Messenger boys such as these in the Phoenix office were busy delivering congratulatory telegrams. (Above) One of the rare surviving photographs of Governor Hunt and his entourage walking to the capitol on Statehood Day shows the governor leading the parade on the right, with his aide Mulford Winsor (in derby) at his left. (Left) An Arizona Gazette (Phoenix) cartoonist drew this sarcastic version of Hunt's walk.

(Following pages) A throng in Prescott on Statehood Day witnessed the planting of a white oak in the town plaza — "The Statehood Tree." The equestrian statue honoring Buckey O'Neill and his Rough Rider comrades is at far left.

Arizona Gazette

Sharlot Hall Museum

Arizona Highways Album 139

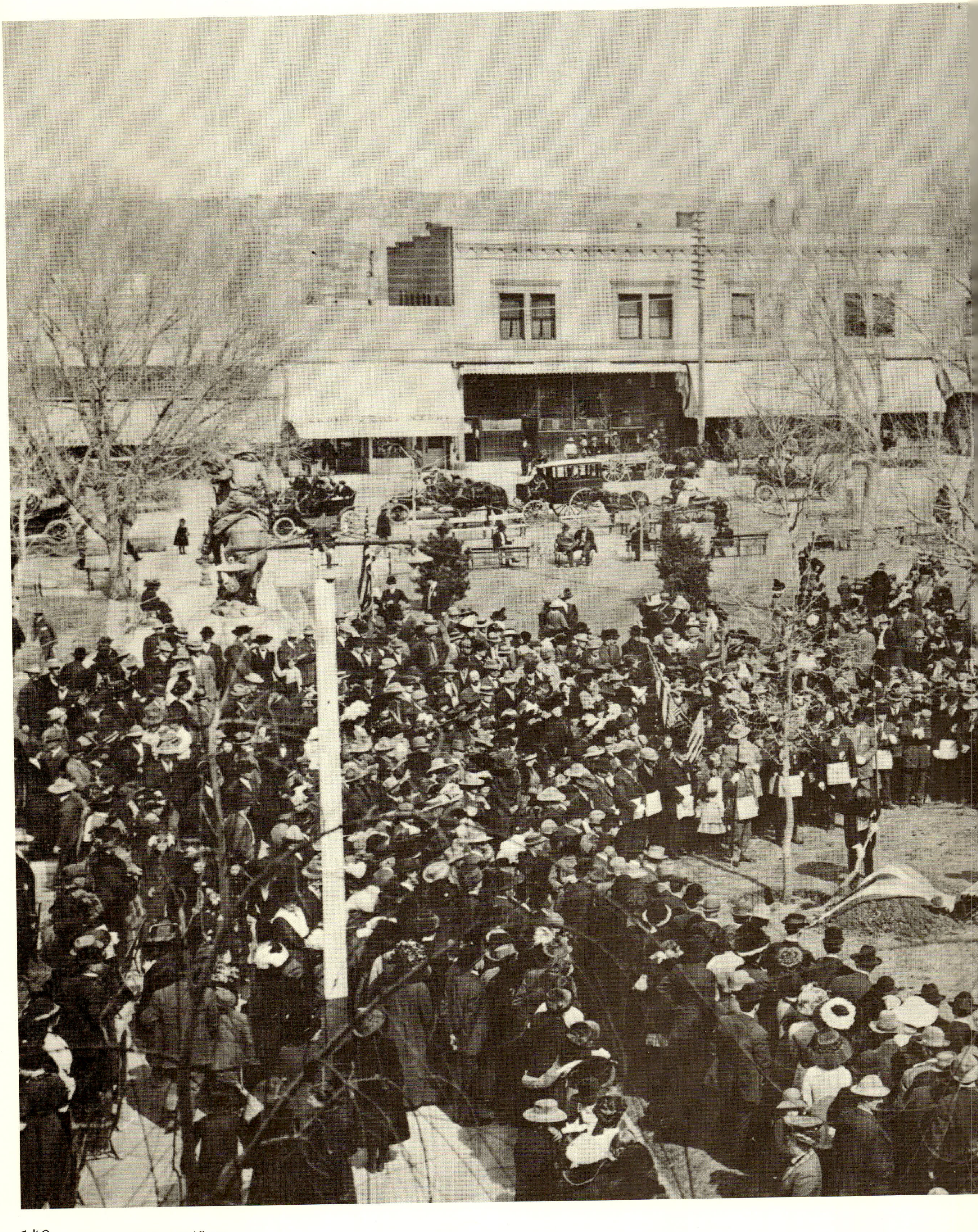

Arizona Highways Album 141

Arizona State Library

McLaughlin Collection

The sun shone brightly on a hushed crowd as the inaugural party mounted the Capitol balcony on the morning of February 14, 1912. (Facing page, top) The words were mostly Mulford Winsor's, but the emotion was Governor George W. P. Hunt's as he promised "a progressive administration" in his inaugural address. (Facing page, bottom) They came on foot and in buggies that day to witness Hunt's swearing-in. Later many of them sat through a two-hour speech by a distinguished visitor, William Jennings Bryan. (Right) Master Barry Goldwater, shown with his father, Baron Goldwater, participated in the new state's first wedding on the morning of Statehood Day.

Goldwater Family Collection

Continued from page 138

militia, from Phoenix Indian School, and from the Tempe Normal School marked time while Hunt skipped around muddy chuckholes beyond the paving, and heaved his bulk across irrigation ditches. In forty-three minutes, the governor-elect covered the fifteen blocks. He climbed the steps to the second floor of the somber pile of granite, tufa, malapai, steel, and zinc — often called the nation's ugliest building — and took the oath of office.

At Hunt's request, no special decorations were evidenced. No honor guard. Just a few flags.

Hunt pledged anew his support of the new state's model constitution, calling it "a beacon light to those states and lands and peoples where the seed of popular government had been sown but not brought forth fruit."

"My administration," he informed his audience of fifteen thousand, "insofar as my conduct can ensure it, will be progressive."

As if to set an example, he went to his office after the inaugural address and put in a respectable part of a day's work.

A reception was followed downtown by street dancing, star pinning, and public displays. Some sort of festival enlivened nearly every Arizona community.

The Phoenix procession began at 1:30, with virtually every patriotic and fraternal organization involved. Band units, fire companies, and school groups passed in review. Sixteen veterans of the Spanish-American War filed by. There followed forty-eight maidens gowned in white and crowned in gold.

A much-publicized cannonade, to consist of forty-eight howitzer salutes on the city hall plaza, so shook window panes and unsettled horses that the booms were halted at thirty-eight. William Jennings Bryan, perennial presidential candidate, more than filled the gap by delivering a two-hour oration.

At the Woman's Club of Phoenix, Miss Hazel Goldberg and Joseph T. Melcer, two of the city's more popular young people, were joined in wedlock. A society reporter observed:

"Master Cupid was indeed present and gallantly guided the bridal party toward the altar, this office being performed by a tiny white-clad figure bearing the name of Master Barry Goldwater...who carried in his arms a bow and quiver of arrows."

That night dancers at the Inaugural Ball reveled shoulder to shoulder in front of the Adams Hotel. As the hour grew late, a hush swept the crowd as a hundred voices of the Phoenix Choral Society sang *a cappella* "The Star Spangled Banner." A photographer had set up his equipment, and, as the music ended, he waved his hand as a signal to extinguish the streetlights.

"Then there was a blinding light and a big boom as the flash powder ignited," wrote a reporter. "Windows rattled and a shower of fire fell, some landing on the arm of the photographer's assistant and burning his arm. Suddenly the governor appeared and a great cheer arose."

Even while the brand-new governor addressed the freshly minted citizens, a reporter for *The Arizona Republican* captured a poignant vignette:

"And, as a short little fellow drew the cinch tight under the belly of his pony, preparing for a long ride back home through the night, he asked of a tall fellow who had already mounted, 'S'pose they have this kinda doin's back in the States?'"

Arizona's big day was done.

DON DEDERA has been delighting Arizonans and all America with his books, articles, and columns for more than 35 years. A former editor of Arizona Highways, *he lives in Phoenix and is currently a free-lance writer. His most recent book,* The Cactus Sandwich, *is a collection of tall tales about Arizona.*

Arizona Highways Album 143

Northern Arizona University Special Collections

And The Bells Rang Out
Continued from page 126

had fiery opposition from *The Arizona Republican*, which called him a Socialist and harped on his ungrammatical speech and writing.

When Hunt spoke in Phoenix while the Ringling Bros. Circus was in town, the *Republican* sneered: "The Honorable G. W. P. Hunt is in town today, and so is the other circus." But when the ballots were counted, Hunt had defeated Wells, 11,123 to 9166.

The Democrats had swept every important office, and they would rule supreme in Arizona for nearly four decades to come.

The race to become America's forty-seventh state had been too close to call until Arizona defied Taft and was forced to take its constitution back to the drawing board. New Mexico had no such problem.

Its constitution makers, meeting in Santa Fe concurrently with the Arizona convention, produced an old-fashioned charter that rejected populist gimmicks and pleased the conservative Taft immensely. "A perfect 1810 model," Arizona historian John R. Murdock later wrote of the New Mexico constitution, contrasting it with Arizona's 1910 approach.

New Mexico's internal tension between the ruling Anglos and the restless Hispanics was aptly illustrated in the name of its convention secretary: George Washington Armijo. When the convention produced the expected conservative constitution, a phalanx of progressives, headed by Albuquerque's Harvey Fergusson, toured the territory in a valiant effort to defeat its passage.

But New Mexico was as eager for statehood as was Arizona. The voters gave the document their approval and sat back to await final action by Congress and the President. Those concurrences were granted without incident, and elections were held.

New Mexico voters chose Albert Fall and Thomas Catron as their first senators, and elected Fergusson and ex-Governor George Curry as their first congressmen. Democrat W. C. McDonald, with the help of rebellious progressive Republicans, scored an upset to win the governor's post.

Taft proclaimed New Mexico the forty-seventh state on January 6, 1912.

"I am glad to give you life," declared the President after signing the New Mexico statehood document.

Until that moment, there had been two territories passionately striving for entry into the mystic Union of American States. Now there was one.

Arizonans were only mildly disappointed at losing their statehood race with New Mexico. They were too busy lining up to seek state jobs, battling for favors, and planning Hunt's inauguration.

Those who dreamed of an elaborate and costly inaugural extravaganza were doomed to disappointment when the plain-living chief executive announced that there would be nothing remotely resembling an imperial coronation. Everything was to be straightforward and economical, just as he said his administration would be.

To symbolize that resolve, he announced he would

walk the fifteen blocks from his hotel to the capitol for his swearing-in — a mammoth feat for a man of his bulk and sedentary habits.

With every muscle screaming out in pain at this unaccustomed torture, Hunt arrived at last at the capitol, where Territorial Governor Sloan was waiting to turn the reins of Arizona government over to him.

"Never again," the new governor must have sworn. Walking was not for him, as evidenced by his immediate hiring of a chauffeured sedan that cost the state's taxpayers $300 per month.

The bells and whistles had been filling the Arizona air with delirious cacophony from the moment when news came over the telegraph that morning of February 14, 1912, that President Taft had just made Arizona the forty-eighth state of the Union.

Even Governor Hunt's wife, the former Helen Duett Ellison, who detested elaborate partying as much as he did, joined in the fun of the Inaugural Ball and resolved to be the dutiful hostess that her lofty new position demanded.

Most of Arizona was still asleep on the morning after the inaugural when Governor Hunt sat down at his new desk. The clock showed a minute after 6:30 A.M.

He had played a leading role in hammering out a state constitution that gave the governor very little power. Now it was time for him to start finding ways to serve effectively within those stringent, self-imposed limits.

Arizona's scenic wonders and mountain playgrounds impressed Congressional investigating committees. Their hosts made certain that the visiting solons enjoyed a side trip to the Grand Canyon (facing page), rode horseback, sampled the cuisine of the new resort hotels, and savored Arizona's famous hospitality. (Top) Visitors and home folks who could not afford expensive hotels could enjoy the Arizona high country in a tent. (Above) Climbing Squaw Peak north of Phoenix was fun, too, but the long skirts of the period made it a real adventure.

Arizona Highways Album   145

(Top) One of the major industries of the Salt River Valley during the first years of statehood was that of raising ostriches. Could a self-respecting cowboy yell, "Git along, little ostrich"? (Center) Harvesting the plumes for ladies' hats required hooding of the surly birds. (Above) As long as the feathers remained fashionable for millinery, the ostrich farms flourished. (Right) These wealthy guests at Castle Hot Springs Resort between Phoenix and Wickenburg enjoyed golf and riding by day, but their plumed hats were on display for evening social functions.

146 Arizona Highways Album

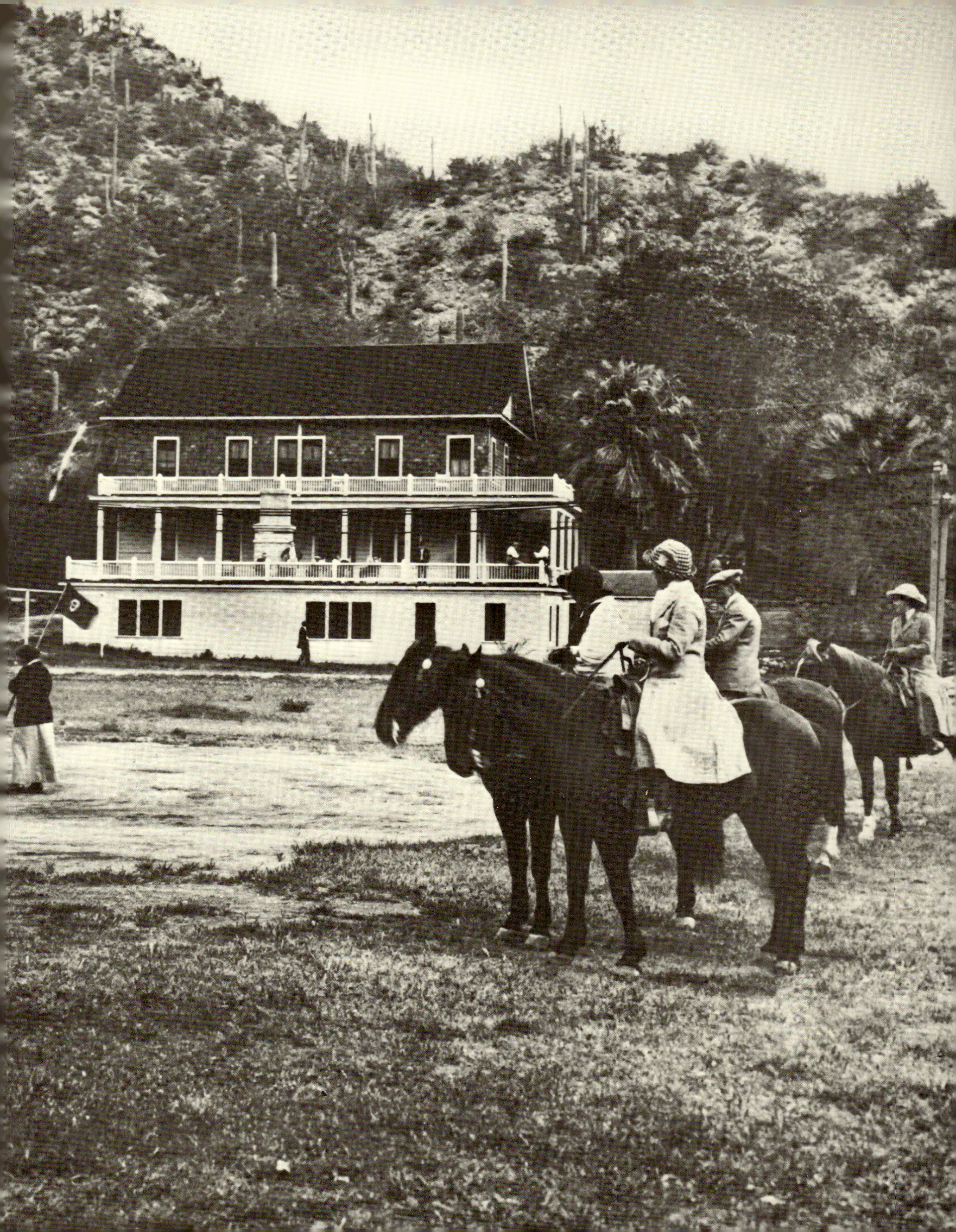

Chapter VI
Launching a New State

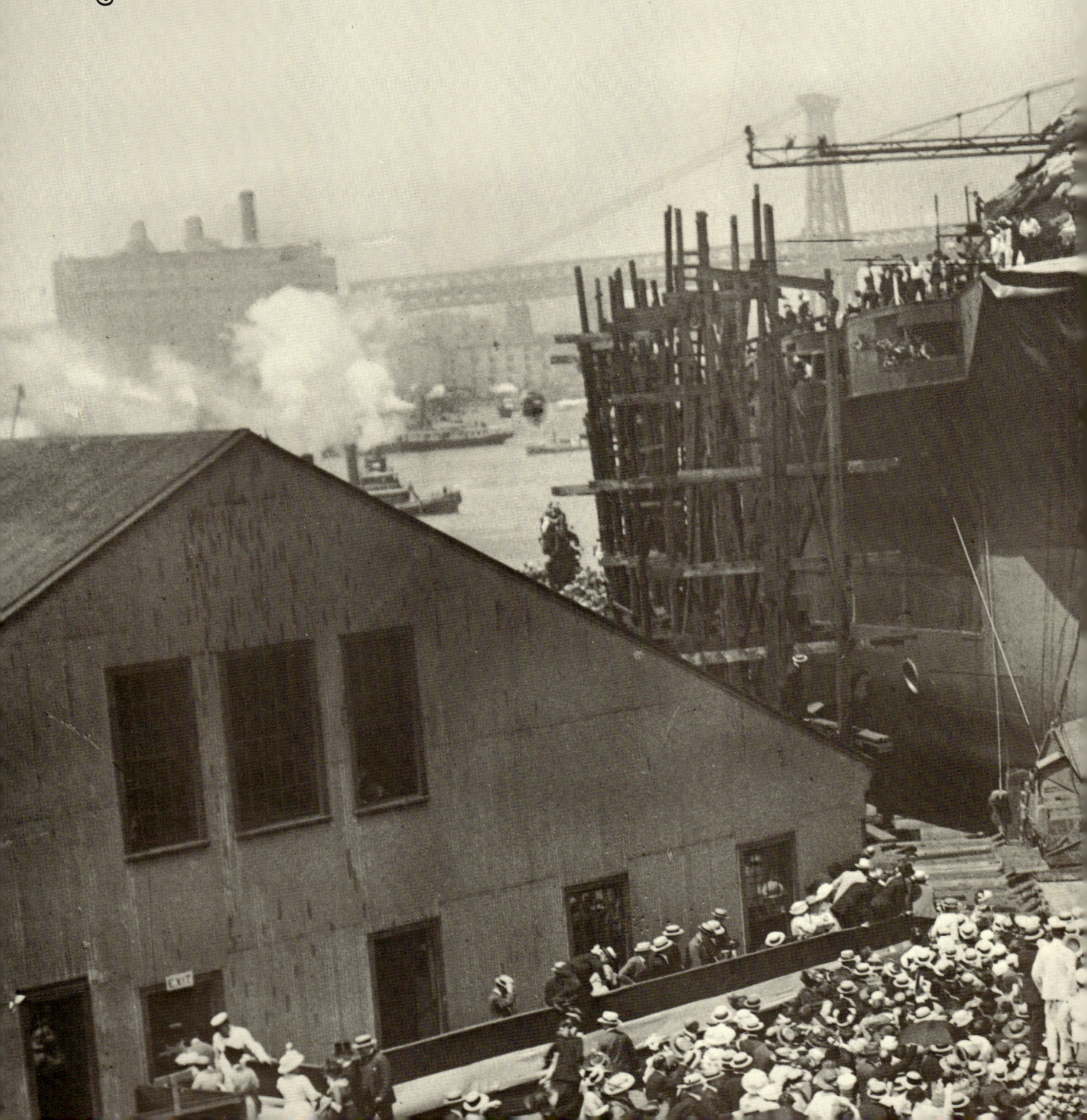

Symbolic of the launching of the new Arizona state government was the launching of the battleship Arizona, *which was christened at Brooklyn Navy Yard on June 19, 1915. Fortunately, this festive crowd could not foresee U.S.S. Arizona's violent death at Pearl Harbor on December 7, 1941.*

Arizona State University Library

McLaughlin Collection

In the euphoria of their statehood celebrations, most Arizonans envisioned a future of uninterrupted growth and prosperity. The big battle had been won and parity with "the States" achieved. From here on, it would be onward and upward.

America had been at peace, except for the brief little Spanish-American War of 1898, for nearly a half-century. Arizonans had almost forgotten that warfare was once a recurring human catastrophe.

Central Arizona was especially blessed in 1912. The miraculous masonry barrier known as Roosevelt Dam, dedicated only a year before, had tamed the unpredictable Salt River and promised never-ending supplies of water to nurture Maricopa County farms and create Maricopa County millionaires.

All around the new state, the future looked bright. Railroading was still a big and profitable business; copper mines poured forth their treasure in Greenlee, Cochise, Yavapai, and Pima counties; lumbering was thriving in Coconino; cattle ranching was enjoying boom times; business was making healthy gains; new tourist resorts were being built, such as Dr. A. J. Chandler's luxurious San Marcos Hotel in the infant town named in his honor.

The 1911-12 *Arizona Business Directory* listed total Arizona population at 204,354 "including 25,000 Indians." The three biggest cities were Tucson, 22,000; Bisbee and suburbs, 16,000; and Phoenix, 15,000. Maricopa County's communities were growing fast: Mesa boasted 2000, Tempe 1600.

It was hard to find a single dark cloud on Arizona's rosy horizon.

But Arizonans were soon to encounter trouble and conflict. Late in 1913, Mexican insurgents along the border struck fear in American hearts and prompted worried Yumans to seek federal troops to guard against marauders. Newspapers of December, 1913, expressed

150   Arizona Highways Album

The new state of Arizona was born in the shadow of conflict. First, Mexican revolutionary Pancho Villa harassed the Arizona border country. Then preparedness for World War I and bloody labor conflict in the mining camps engrossed Arizonans. (Upper left) Flags waved bravely at patriotic rallies across the state. (Above) First Arizona State Legislature, meeting in 1912 and 1913, faced a backbreaking agenda. The Senate is shown in session here.

Arizona Highways Album

Bisbee Mining and Historical Museum

deep concern about a new war with Mexico.

Not many months thereafter, Pancho Villa's exuberant followers clashed with American infantry at Nogales, Sonora. In March of 1916, Villa crossed the border and raided Columbus, New Mexico.

Meanwhile, Europe had erupted into full-scale war in August, 1914, and America was sucked ever closer to that deadly conflict, despite the neutrality efforts of President Woodrow Wilson.

Within weeks after United States entry into the World War in April, 1917, Arizona faced serious internal conflict in the form of mine strike violence. The radical International Workers of the World seized leadership in the strike effort, and, on July 6, furious Jerome residents drove sixty-three striking militants from their city. A week later, Bisbee officials hastily deputized scores of men to force 1100 strikers into freight cars and send them heading east to New Mexico.

Arizona's Old West vigilante spirit was still alive and well.

The state became a vast military training area as her sons answered the call for service "Over There" in 1917. Aviation was forced to grow up in a hurry to meet wartime demands, and the state produced one of America's great flying aces in Lieutenant Frank Luke, Jr., who met a hero's death in the skies over France.

It was against this backdrop of conflict and turmoil that Arizona struggled to put a new state government on track.

The new state officials took over unfamiliar duties in unfamiliar offices and attempted to chart political courses with few precedents. Governor Hunt was besieged by applicants for positions on boards and commissions, and other elected officials worked overtime to get their departments functioning. It was a capable crew: Sidney P. Osborn, secretary of state; George P. Bullard, attorney general; David Johnson, state treasurer; John C. Callaghan, state auditor; and Charles O. Case, superintendent of public instruction.

Even busier were members of the First Arizona State Legislature, which had only sixty days in which to chart a new legislative course for the state. With Sam Bradner of Benson as speaker of the House of Representatives and Michael Cuniff of Prescott presiding over the Senate, the legislators met on March 18, 1912, and were administered the oath of office by Alfred Franklin, chief justice of the Supreme Court. Then they squirmed for two hours while Governor Hunt read his 18,000-word message to the legislature — one of the longest on record.

Hunt soon learned a lesson that Arizona chief

152 Arizona Highways Album

Organized labor flexed its muscles during the early years of Arizona statehood. Flushed with victory in the 1911 elections, labor leaders pressed for better pay and working conditions in the copper mines. (Left) As violence flared, many citizens, such as this worried Bisbee man and his family, started carrying guns.

(Below) When the radical International Workers of the World grabbed control of mine strikes in 1917, angry townspeople loaded strikers onto railroad cars and shipped them out of Arizona. This photograph shows the Bisbee deportation. (Lower right) Labor unrest boiled in mining communities across the state.

Bisbee Mining and Historical Museum

Arizona Historical Society, Tucson

executives have been relearning for seventy-five years: The legislature rarely, if ever, is obedient to the wishes of the governor.

"The lower house has fallen into the hands of the special interests!" Hunt fumed to a friend on one of his more frustrating days.

The lawmakers ground out a prodigious number of bills, but Hunt was not satisfied. He called them back into special session immediately after adjournment, and, in early 1913, he called them back twice more.

By that time, the voters had put the controversial recall provision back into the constitution; had granted the vote to women; and were soon (1914) to make Prohibition the law of the state, a fact which only made liquor a little more inconvenient to obtain.

The First Arizona Legislature was an earnest, hard-working body, and a big-spending one, by 1912 standards. It shocked the conservative press by passing a state budget of almost half a million dollars.

Governor Hunt, who battled for every piece of liberal legislation and cried out for more, took his record to the voters in the first state election in 1914. Although he was opposed by popular Republican Ralph Cameron, Hunt won easily, with some 25,000 votes to Cameron's 17,000-plus.

Continued on page 168

Arizona Highways Album

Salt River Project

Desert Caballeros Museum

Arizona Historical Society, Tucson

In most Arizona communities, the business of making a living went on as usual. (Upper left) In Tempe, the Princess Bakery (or was it Princes?) made bread under misspelled signs. (Center left) A new-fangled truck replaced the horse-drawn wagon for the Arizona Highway Department at Wickenburg. (Lower left) F. Ronstadt's Hardware thrived in Tucson. (Above) Peters Grocery in Phoenix was a model of neatness. (Right) Everybody worked hard and, like this shoeshine boy, took sleep where one could find it.

State Government At Last

By Jay J. Wagoner

Now that Arizona was safely in the Union, it was time for Governor George W. P. Hunt to preside over the launching of the new state government.

Hunt was to be the dominant political figure during the first twenty years of statehood. Elected governor seven times during that span, he was called "his hereditary governorship" by the famous Will Rogers.

Hunt was a strong personal leader—just what Arizona needed for its first governor, because the new state constitution gave little power to the chief executive's office. Though he was a wealthy man, Hunt identified politically with the common people and with organized labor during the early part of his tenure as governor. Hunt was philosophically a progressive reformer and visionary but also a practical politician of the old school. He traveled frequently around the state by automobile to mingle with the voters, building a loyal political machine based largely on patronage jobs in the State Highway Department.

The purpose of the American progressive movement at the beginning of the twentieth century was to achieve needed social and economic reforms by making government more responsive to the needs of the people. Arizona was one of the first states to put the initiative, referendum, and, later, the recall into the hands of the voters. Arizonans wasted no time getting involved in direct democracy, taking prompt action on progressive measures left undone by the constitutional convention.

Male voters went to the polls and approved suffrage for women in 1912, eight years before the United States Constitution was amended to give women the vote nationwide. Two years later, the electorate outlawed the blacklist, a weapon used by corporations to keep workers in line. Up with the people; down with the special interests—the signs of progressive reform were there.

The people voted to make Arizona a dry state. On New Year's Eve, 1914, thousands of Arizonans gathered in the streets, saloons, and churches. Some folks were out for a final fling; others ushered in the new era of Prohibition with rejoiceful prayer.

The issue of capital punishment was on the ballot in three successive elections. The voters endorsed the death penalty, then replaced it with life imprisonment, and finally restored capital punishment by a two-to-one vote. Governor Hunt was disappointed. During the campaigns, he had compared hanging to the "burning of witches."

Hunt not only opposed the death penalty but also had other humanitarian ideas on the treatment of criminals. He eliminated striped uniforms and put prisoners to work on state roads and bridges. On one occasion he hosted convict laborers at a Tempe restaurant, and he received national press coverage when he spent a night in a prison cell at Arizona State Prison in Florence.

With Governor Hunt riding the wave of social reform that swept through the nation, and the people voting directly on critical issues, Arizona appeared to be in the vanguard of the progressive movement.

But was it?

Hunt was well aware that he had little power as governor to reform Arizona the way he wanted to. Much to his regret, the constitution that he helped write made the executive a "headless branch of government." The governor, only the first among equals in a multiple executive system, had no control over the five other elected executive officers.

The governor also was given little authority over numerous agencies, boards, and commissions created by the legislature. The lawmakers often ignored his budget recommendations for these groups. Is it any wonder the bureaucracy looked to the legislature rather than to the governor for direction?

"The legislature," as one political observer explained, "regards the governor as a foolish nincompoop who was written into the Constitution by mistake."

The legislature was made the strongest branch of state government, and every Arizona legislature has accepted this role happily. Governor Hunt, a master of strategy in some aspects of political life, never developed any special skill in dealing with the legislature. There was little party loyalty in a one-party state. With no viable opposition, the Democrats split into factions rather than working as a bloc.

As early as 1913, Governor Hunt branded his fellow Democrats in the legislature as "reactionary" and a "do-nothing body." His opponents answered in kind, describing him as "strong-willed, uncompromising, and righteously independent." Hunt was especially irked because the lawmakers passed a penal code over his veto. The code authorized the death penalty and took away the governor's power to grant a pardon without the approval of the new Board of Pardons and Paroles. The penal code was approved by the voters when it was submitted to them as a referendum.

By the end of Hunt's first term, a pattern of conflict had developed between the governor's office and the legislature that would continue during most of the state's history.

Hunt often said that the legislators did what the big copper companies, railroads, and ranchers told them to do. During the first half-century of statehood, these big economic interests probably had greater influence on legislative activities than the governor, the political parties, and even the people. The people didn't complain much because many jobs and businesses depended on the prosperity of the mines, ranches, farms, and railroads.

Arizona's economic and political climates did not change greatly until after World War II, when thousands of people began moving from other states to the urban areas of Phoenix and Tucson. Manufacturing then surged ahead of copper, cattle, and cotton to become the leading industry. A two-party system developed in the 1950s as many newcomers registered Republican. Conservative Democrats identified with the new image of Republican success and began switching parties. Today, either party can win a statewide election.

The legislature remained continuously in Democratic hands, except for the loss of the state senate for one term, until 1966. In that year, the United States Supreme Court mandated reapportionment on the basis of one man, one vote. Control of the legislature then passed from rural conservative Democrats to urban conservative Republicans, who were elected mainly in the Phoenix area where more than half the people lived.

The new lawmakers streamlined state government by combining dozens of agencies into super-departments, each headed by a director accountable to the governor. This long-awaited reform strengthened the office of governor.

Looking back, it is obvious that the new state government was launched with handicaps—a weak governor's office, a legislature beholden to special interests, and a one-party system. From the perspective of seventy-five years, we also can see that Arizona flirted with progressivism and then chose conservatism as its partner.

JAY J. WAGONER, for many years a teacher in the Phoenix Union High School system, is the author of six books on Arizona history. His Arizona Territory, 1863-1912, a Political History, *is a classic in the field. A former Fulbright Scholar, he has traveled the world seeking the roots of history.*

Statehood brought many changes to progressive Arizona. (Facing page) Suffragette parades, such as this march in Yuma, promoted the cause of votes for women, which Arizona men voted into law in 1912, eight years before America did so. (Above) Arizona was ahead of the nation with Prohibition, too. Liquor was made illegal in 1914, but bootleggers supplied the thirsty masses, despite lawmen's raids such as this one in Clifton in 1915.

Arizona was moving rapidly into the modern era, but the gracious charm of Victorian days departed reluctantly. (Above) This Mesa home was built for pleasant living. (Upper right) There were still over-decorated parlors, with ornately carved furniture and (lower right) photo nooks presided over by the beloved Teddy Roosevelt.

158   Arizona Highways Album

McLaughlin Collection

Mesa Southwest Museum

Jack Dykinga

McLaughlin Collection

McLaughlin Collection

Not all the ladies were marching for the right to vote. (Top) Some tended beautiful gardens at handsome homes in Phoenix. (Above) Some ventured out of the parlor to wash the family Model-T Ford, like this one in Scottsdale. (Right) And others gathered in sewing bees. This was a scene at the Bisbee YWCA.

(Following pages) That grand old hostelry of Apache County, the Barth Hotel at St. Johns, was a landmark for travelers over a span of decades. Sol Barth, one of the early pioneers of northeastern Arizona, was still proprietor of the hotel when this motorcade passed through St. Johns.

McLaughlin Collection

Bisbee Mining and Historical Museum

Arizona Highways Album   161

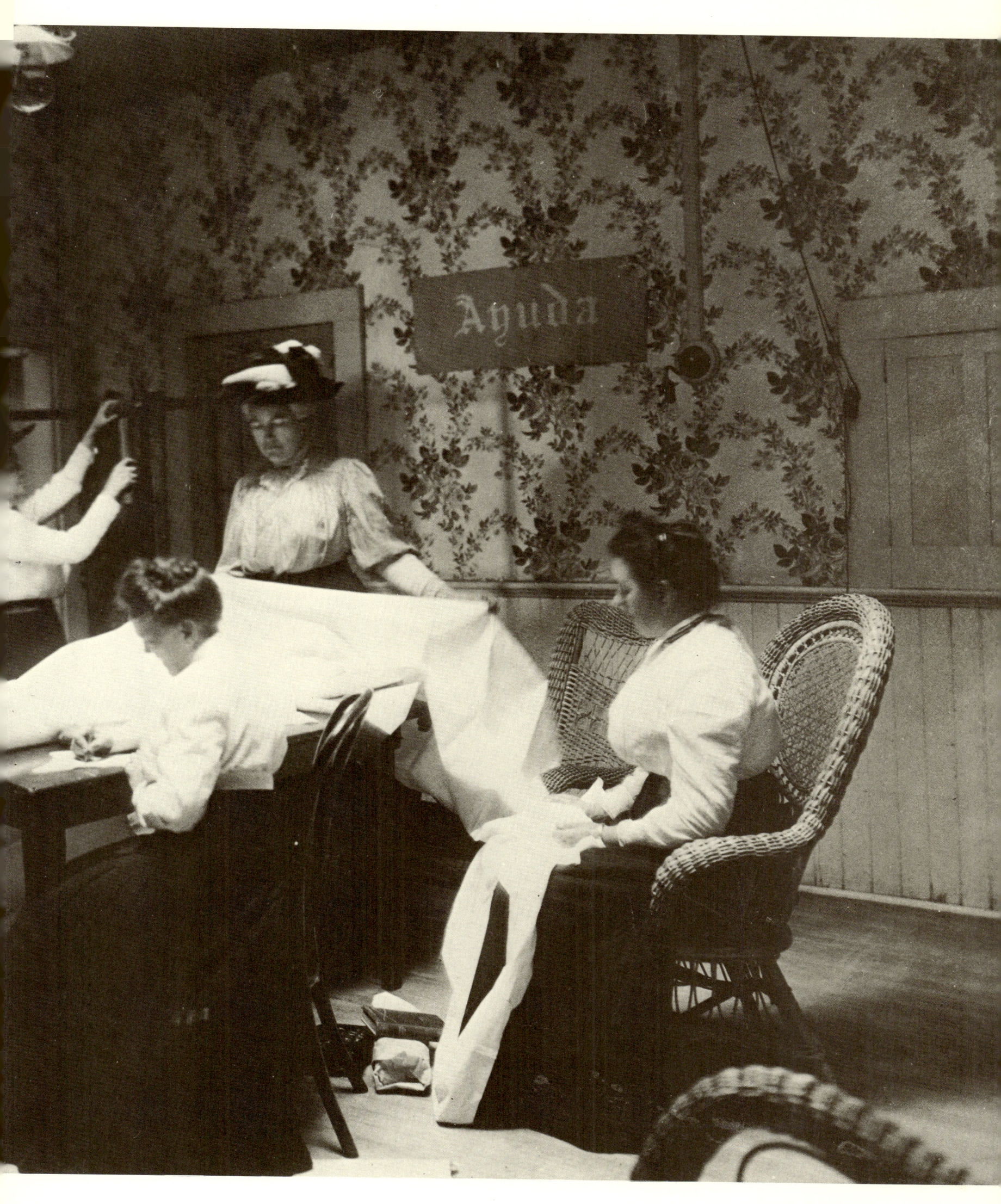

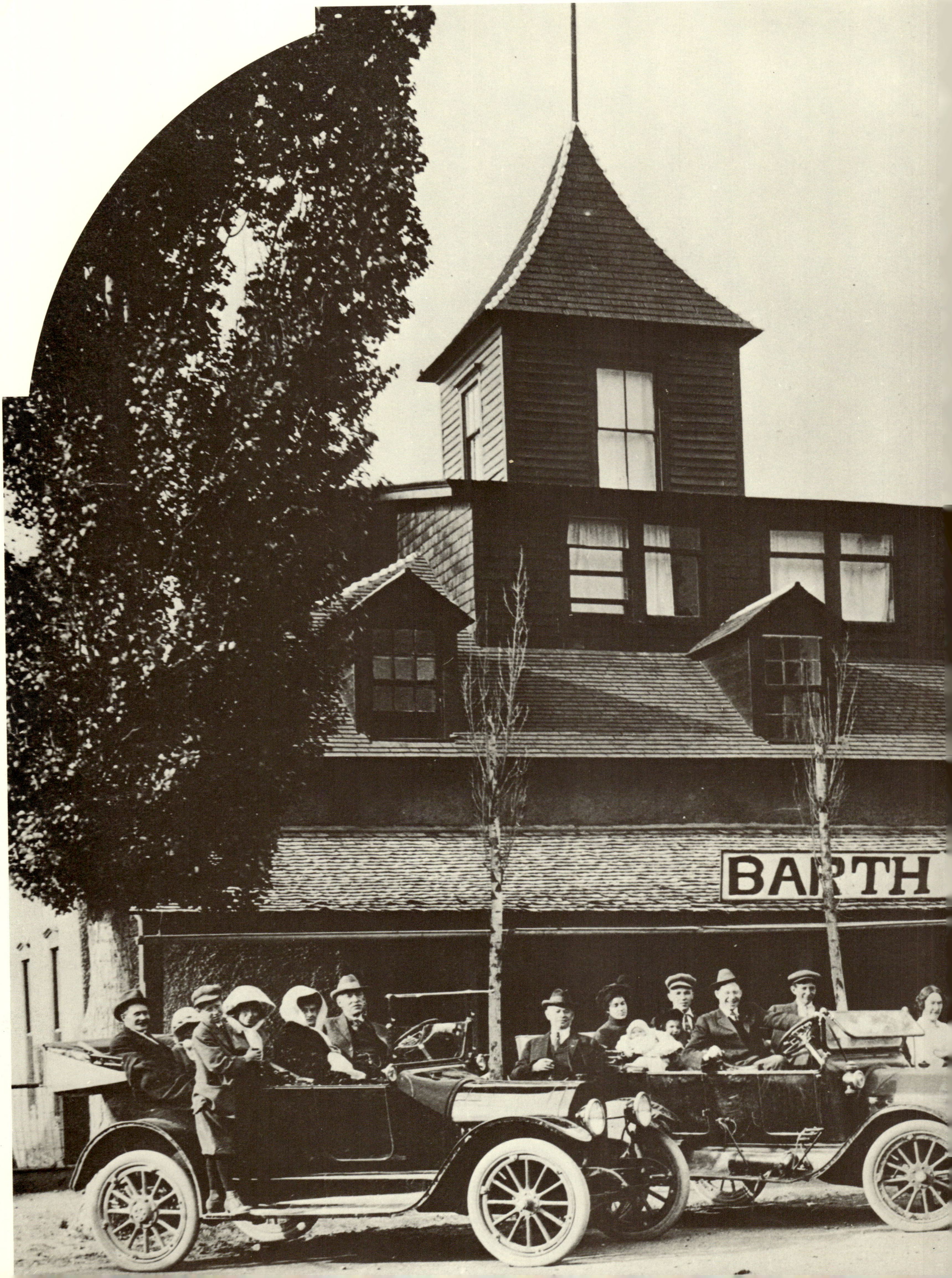
BARTH

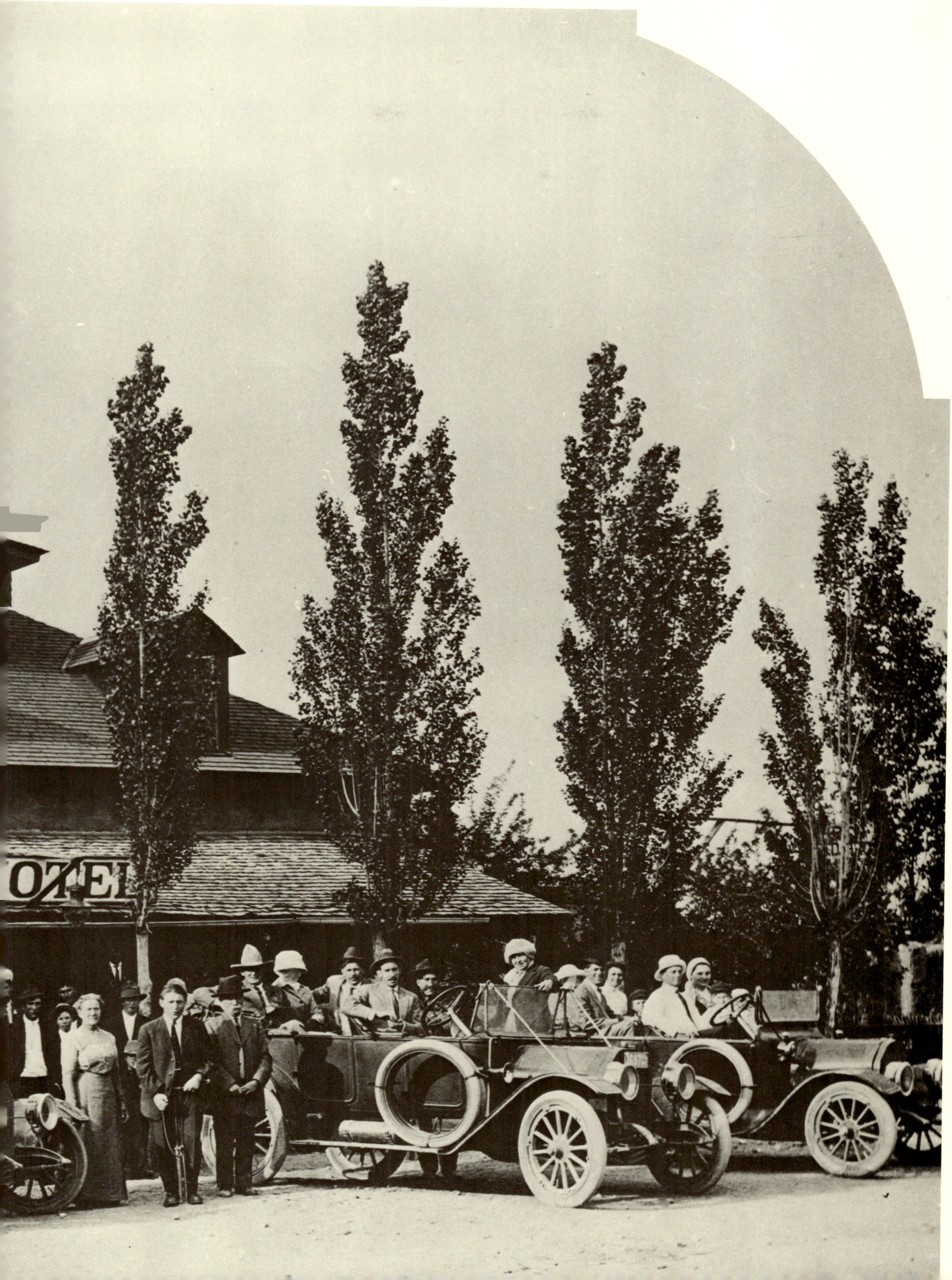
OTEL

Incomparable George W. P. Hunt

By Dean Smith

He loved to be called "the Old Roman," but George W. P. Hunt's detractors had other names for him.

Some thought his bulgy body and massive mustache made "Old Walrus" more appropriate. Others called him "portly," "owlish," "illiterate," "baldy," "conniving." Still other sobriquets were unprintable.

But nobody ever called Hunt stupid, lazy, or incompetent.

Certainly his supporters far outnumbered his enemies. The "George Washington" of his new state — president of the constitutional convention and first chief executive — was unquestionably the major political figure in Arizona during the first two decades of statehood. Seven times the voters elected him their governor, a record that is virtually certain to stand forever, now that Arizona grants its chief executive a four-year term. There have been few more colorful or controversial figures.

George Wiley Paul Hunt was born November 1, 1859, at Huntsville, Missouri, the son of a California '49er father and a mother who wrote poetry for *Godey's Lady's Book*. The restless youth left home at eighteen and made his way westward in railroad boxcars to seek his fortune. He did not bother to inform his distraught parents of his plans; so for five years they feared he had been scalped by Indians.

For more than three years, he bummed around Colorado and New Mexico mining camps; then, in 1881, he heard that the mines were booming at Globe, in Arizona Territory. Early in October of that year he walked into Globe almost penniless, wearing dirty overalls and escorting a burro that carried his few possessions.

That same day, he got a job as a waiter at Pascoe's Restaurant, and for the next three years his routine varied only slightly: rise long before dawn to read any available book, report for work at 5 A.M., labor at the restaurant until 8 P.M., and read another hour before bedtime.

In 1890, at age thirty, Hunt became a delivery boy and clerk for the store that soon became the Old Dominion Commercial Company. In classic Horatio Alger fashion, he rose to the presidency of that large firm within a decade.

The earnest young man with the owlish glasses first ran for office in Arizona in 1890, when he was defeated in the race for Gila County recorder. He ran for the territorial legislature in 1892, and this time he won.

During a political career that spanned four decades, Hunt was to enjoy amazing success. He soon became a power in the Arizona House of Representatives, and, in 1896, he was elected to the Council (Senate) of the legislature. When Arizona headed down the homestretch of its race for statehood, Hunt served as president of the Council in the territorial legislatures of 1905 and 1909.

As the recognized leader of the Progressive Democrats, who espoused the cause of the laboring man against the entrenched corporations, he was the popular choice for president of the labor-dominated Arizona constitutional convention of 1910.

Despite the opposition of several powerful newspapers, including his hometown *Globe Silver Belt*, he scored an easy victory in the election for Arizona's first state governor in December, 1911. He

164 Arizona HIGHWAYS Album

Arizona State Library

Governor Hunt often appeared in public in rumpled white suits, but he could dress up (facing page) for a formal portrait. He was willing to be photographed for any good cause—or no cause at all. In this rare picture, (left) the chief executive of Arizona is knitting, presumably to set an example for World War I home-front conservation. The flag and President Woodrow Wilson's photograph are in the background.

was re-elected so regularly that he came to regard the governorship as his personal property. Aside from a period of service as U. S. minister to Siam in 1920-21 and two brief Republican breakthroughs, Hunt sat in the governor's chair until Dr. B. B. Moeur ousted him in the Democratic primary of 1932.

The "Old Roman" made one last bid for the governorship in 1934, and when he failed, he clung to life only three months thereafter. To him, there was no meaningful existence outside of public service.

George W. P. Hunt was a fascinating blend of lofty idealism and practical power politics.

When Hunt died, on Christmas Eve, 1934, Senator Carl Hayden declared that his career had been one of "picturesque courage," and that he had "wielded more influence on the political life of the state than any other man."

Few could argue with that.

DEAN SMITH has lived in Arizona for more than half a century. He has been a newspaper reporter, university administrator, free-lance writer, and executive vice president of the Arizona Historical Foundation. A resident of Tempe, he has been writing about Arizona's heritage for several decades. His most recent book is The Goldwaters of Arizona.

Arizona Highways Album   165

McLaughlin Collection

McLaughlin Collection

Arizona State Library

Arizona fell madly in love with automobiles during the early years of statehood. (Upper left) Even when they collapsed in a heap, or (center left) blew out all four tires at once, or (lower left) had to be ferried over a river — the Gila River at Florence in this instance — everybody admired the tin lizzies of the day. In this transition stage between the horse and the auto, the blacksmith shops became garages. (Above) The Reliable Auto and Blacksmith Shop in Flagstaff was ready for anything. (Right) Phoenix and Tucson became early auto racing centers, attracting stars like the famed Barney Oldfield, at left, to local speed events.

Arizona Historical Society, Tucson

Launching a New State
Continued from page 153

As Arizona entered its third year of statehood, the patterns of the future were already taking shape. Gone or fast disappearing, but still lamented by some, were the wild days of the past: the saloon shoot-outs and wide-open red-light districts; frontier justice, enforced by the six-gun and the lynching rope; the era of the free and open range, the simple times when disputes were settled without phalanxes of lawyers and a man's handshake was his contract.

Statehood and civilization were mixed blessings in the eyes of those who remembered when they, and Arizona Territory, were young.

The coming of the automobile was revolutionizing travel in the new state. Now a family could motor from Safford to Phoenix in a day or two, even with several stops en route to change tires or repair a balky engine. The famed plank road across the desert sands west of Yuma enabled motorists to cut driving time to the cool beaches of San Diego, California. Imaginative engineers were drawing plans for good highways over such rugged routes as Yarnell Hill, near Prescott, and Salt River Canyon, in east-central Arizona.

Now flying daredevils were barnstorming at county fairs, and some visionaries were dreaming of passenger travel by air. No longer isolated, the Baby State was in instantaneous contact via telegraph with the financial centers of the nation. Some wealthy visitors to Castle Hot Springs resort went so far as to have stock tickers installed in their vacation cottages. Moving picture companies were planning to film Westerns in the state. Soon the discovery of radio would have youngsters scrambling to build crystal sets. The invention of new wonders, it seemed, would never cease.

For Arizonans, looking confidently to the brightest of futures, it was already becoming hard to remember those primitive territorial years before February, 1912, when statehood was only an improbable dream.

Arizona Historical Society, Tucson

Arizona's highway system developed rapidly to serve the new state's widely separated cities. Many a formidable natural barrier was conquered by the highway engineers. (Upper left) The plank road over the shifting desert sands west of Yuma provided turn-out stations so motorists could pass. (Above) The mighty Colorado River had been bridged at Yuma before, but never so efficiently as by this nearly completed automobile bridge.

McLaughlin Collection

McLaughlin Collection

Aviation and America's entrance into World War I captured the attention of all Arizonans. In 1918 the young state's flying daredevil, Lt. Frank Luke of Phoenix (above, second from right) shot down nine German airplanes and twelve observation balloons during an amazing seventeen-day combat career before being killed. Luke's statue stands in front of the Arizona capitol today, and Luke Air Force Base is a living memorial to him. (Right) Women served in many capacities on the home front, many as nurses. (Facing page) The nattily uniformed First Arizona Regiment rifle team brought honor to the state.

170 Arizona Highways Album

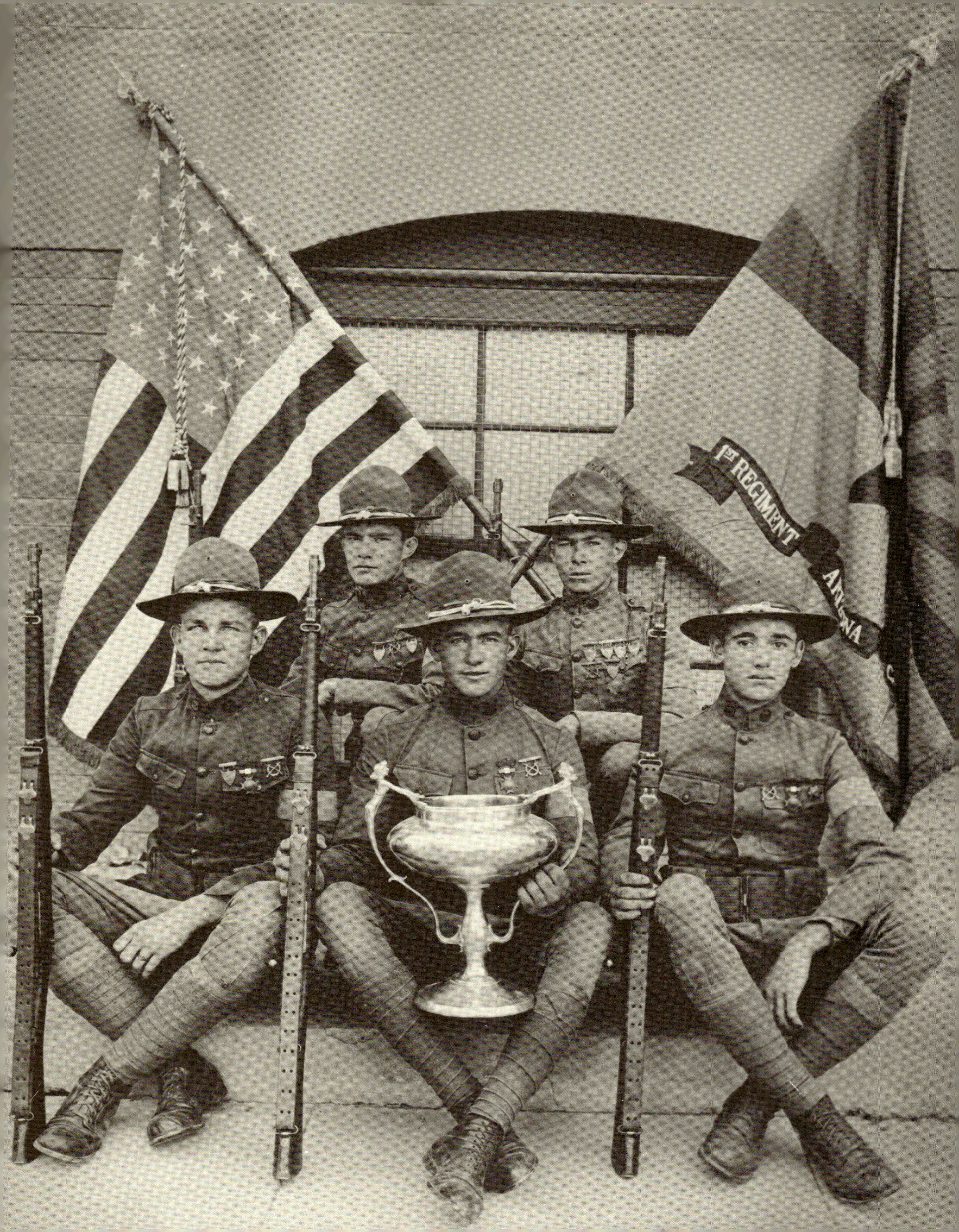
1ST REGIMENT

Chapter VII
After Seventy-five Years

Gazing from the plush Golden Eagle dining room atop the forty-four-story Valley Bank Center, you can look down on well over a million citizens of Phoenix and the Salt River Valley at work or play. Less than two hours to the south by freeway, approximately 400,000 Tucsonans are enjoying a technicolored Arizona sunset.

All across the state, cities of 20,000 and more are growing and thriving. Modern highways make all Arizonans close neighbors and sharers in the wonders of today's technology.

Vast acreages of concrete parking lots surround semiconductor plants and shopping malls, displacing the alfalfa fields and cattle feeding lots that once enriched Arizona's economy. Boisterous mining camps are silent ghost towns now, and lawmen in three-piece suits track high-tech criminals who rob with computers instead of six-guns.

Sun City and Green Valley retirement communities now number more residents than the combined populations of Bisbee, Douglas, Jerome, and all the ranches in Yavapai and Coconino counties. Youngsters who spend their allowances on video games will grow to old age without ever throwing a leg over a horse.

This is Arizona, 1987 — a fantasyland which could not even be imagined in the most feverish dreams of Marcus Smith or George W. P. Hunt. The old has vanished, and the new is here to stay, bringing smog and traffic jams to counterbalance the joys of word processors and microwave ovens.

It seems incredible to us now, but, only seventy-five years ago, this raw territory was widely considered too primitive for statehood. It is almost as hard to believe that many of the youngsters who celebrated on Arizona's Statehood Day are still with us to toast her Diamond Jubilee.

How have we grown since the bells rang out on Statehood Day?

Perhaps the most spectacular measure is that of population, which has been doubling every twenty or thirty years since 1912.

The first big surge of immigration came in 1945-50, when men who had taken military training in Arizona returned by the thousands after World War II. The 1960 census revealed that 1,302,161 citizens called Arizona home in that year. Today's unofficial estimates show Arizona's population approaching 3,500,000, and the boom continues unabated.

One of the consequences of the Great Migration, much of it at the expense of upper Midwest states, was the strengthening of the Republican Party in Arizona. Howard Pyle broke the Democrats' stranglehold on the governorship when he became the state's chief executive in 1950. Barry Goldwater's Senate victory and John Rhodes' successful bid for a House seat, both in 1952, provided further evidence that the Republicans had come to stay.

Today Arizona is still conservative country, but both major parties are alive and well.

And how the economy has changed! As recently as thirty years ago, the "three C's" — copper, cattle, and cotton (some added climate and citrus) were still the major producers of Arizona wealth. But even at that time the influence of the mining corporations and the big ranchers had waned, along with that of the railroad magnates. Manufacturing — smokeless, high-tech manufacturing — moved into the state and became the biggest employer. Tourism now rivals all other Arizona industries, and the new resort complexes are among the most luxurious in the nation. Retirees, settling in an amazing variety of planned communities, pour millions of dollars into the economy each month.

Agriculture still occupies an important place in the scheme of things, but that importance diminishes with each transformation of farmland into office buildings or housing developments. One notable exception to the retreat of agriculture is in Yuma County, where million-dollar orange groves perfume the clean desert

Arizona Highways Album

air and turn the brown landscape to brilliant green. In all of Arizona's fifteen counties (La Paz on the Colorado River has recently joined the fourteen that greeted Arizona statehood), farming thrives wherever there is a river valley, an electric pump, or proximity to the miracle of irrigation.

A struggling frontier university and two tiny normal schools did not convince graduates of Harvard or Columbia that Arizona in 1912 had the educational resources requisite to responsible statehood. Neither did an occasional itinerant performer's visit to a Tombstone theater impress habitues of the Met and Carnegie Hall. To most of "civilized" America, Arizona entered the Union as a cultural wasteland.

Moreover, they asked, where are Arizona's statesmen? It might well be half a century, critics speculated in 1912, before the cactus country could produce a political leader of national stature.

They could hardly have imagined that Arizona would one day boast three excellent state universities, community colleges in all parts of the state, and many private educational institutions. It seemed impossible that this frontier land could become a center of astronomy, or that the world's great symphony orchestras would perform in Arizona's renowned concert halls.

And who could have known in 1912 that newly elected Henry Fountain Ashurst and Carl Hayden were destined to become giants in the U.S. Senate? Arizona has been producing far more than its share of national political figures ever since.

What irresistible magnets continue to lure new residents to Arizona from all the other forty-nine states and many foreign nations?

In 1912 they came to build their fortunes in a new land of opportunity, shrugging off the privations of frontier life in the hope of a brighter future.

Today they flock into Arizona for different reasons: the much-touted relaxed life-style; the sunny climate, now made bearable during desert summers by modern air conditioning; the glories of Arizona's scenic wonders; ideal conditions for active retirement; the promise of jobs in an economy that always seems to elude depression.

All these are sensible and valid reasons for moving to Arizona. But they may not be the principal reasons. It is just possible that the lure of the Wild West lingers on, and that the mystique of the frontier—the exotic land of room enough and time enough—grows stronger with each passing decade.

After all, there are still cowboys riding the Arizona range; colorfully costumed Hopi Indians on their ancient mesas, dancing with religious fervor as rattlesnakes hang from their mouths; remote canyons and forests and peaks that rarely have felt the step of man.

And another thing: Nobody has yet found the Lost Dutchman's fabled gold mine in the mystery-shrouded Superstition Mountains.

Arizona joined the brotherhood of American states on February 14, 1912, but it did not give up its unique individuality. The Wild West syndrome, an obstacle to statehood for so long, lingers today, and it gives Arizona an allure that Iowa or New Jersey or Alabama will never know.

Arizona Today

POPULATION
State total — 3,263,000

Largest counties
- Maricopa — 1,860,000
- Pima — 638,000
- Pinal — 104,000
- Cochise — 95,300
- Yuma — 89,200

(The *Arizona Business Directory* for 1911-1912, the year Arizona achieved statehood, shows Arizona Territory had a population of 204,354. Cochise County had the largest population, 34,600, but was being overtaken by Maricopa County, with 34,500. The next most populous counties were Yavapai, Pima, and Graham, in that order.)

Largest cities
- Phoenix — 866,680
- Tucson — 377,545
- Mesa — 191,380
- Tempe — 143,970
- Glendale — 117,150

(Arizona Territory's largest cities at the start of 1912 were: Tucson, 22,000; Bisbee and suburbs, 16,000; Phoenix, 15,000; Douglas, 10,000; Prescott, 5,100.)

MAJOR INCOME PRODUCERS (millions of dollars)
- Manufacturing (value added) — $7,550
- Tourism and travel — 5,180
- Mineral production — 1,483
- Crop production — 830
- Livestock production — 767

EMPLOYMENT
- Wholesale, retail trade — 301,200
- Services and miscellaneous — 296,200
- Manufacturing — 182,800
- State, local government — 163,500
- Construction — 111,100

AGE DISTRIBUTION
- 29 and younger — 1,602,000
- 30-64 — 1,263,000
- 65 and older — 398,000

MEDIAN FAMILY INCOME (1980 census)
- Statewide — $19,017
- Highest counties (before mine closings)
  - Greenlee — 22,661
  - Maricopa — 20,478
  - Pima — 19,000
  - Coconino — 18,100
  - Pinal — 16,286

SOURCES OF NEWCOMERS (since 1980)
- California — 87,000
- New Mexico — 29,000
- Illinois — 28,500
- Texas — 26,000
- Michigan — 23,500

1985 figures unless otherwise indicated. (Sources: Arizona Statistical Review, 1985, Valley National Bank of Arizona; Arizona Department of Commerce.)

J. Peter Mortimer

San Xavier Mission near Tucson, a jewel of Arizona's past and present, will be a treasure for centuries to come.

Index

Italic page numbers denote illustrations.

A

Adams Hotel: *112*, 143
Ajo: 52
Allen, Butch: 99
Alvord, Burt: 36
Amado, Demetrio: 28
Apache marauders: 35
Apache Trail: *118*, 121
Apache woman: *13*
Arizona:
    Capitol Building: *76-77*, 96, 137, *142*
    General information: 172-174
    Rangers: 36, *37*
    State Prison: *156*
    Territorial Prison: *32-33*
Arizona Republican: 111, 122, 131, 143
Armijo, George Washington: 144
Ashurst, Henry Fountain: *50*, 126, *127*, 173

B

Babbitt Brothers: 19
Baker, Albert C.: 108, *110*
Bailey, Joseph: 100
Bard, Thomas B.: 86
Barth Hotel: *162-163*
Benson Union High School: *69*
Beveridge, Albert J.: 82, *82*, 86, 87, 96, 130-131
Bisbee: 22, 27, 43, 52, 78, *80-81*, 82, *102*, 131, *135*, *136*, 138, 150, 152, *153*, *160-161*, 172
Boer War: 52
Boys Brigade: *45*
Bradner, Sam: 152
Breckenridge, William: 116-117
Brewery Gulch: *84*
Brodie, Alexander O.: 56
Brooks, Johnnie: 38
Bryan, William Jennings: 143
Buckeye: *132*
Bullard, George P.: 152

C

Callaghan, John C.: 152
Camelback Mountain: *104-105*
Cameron, Ralph: *125*, 126, 131, *131*, 153
Camp Whipple: *17*, 40, *41*
Carson, Kit: 40
Carlisle Indians: 73
Casa Grande Ruins: *86*
Case, Charles O.: 152
Castle Hot Springs Resort: *146-147*, 168
Catron, Thomas: 144
Celaya, Carmen: 28
Chacon, Augustine: 36
Chandler, A.J.: 150

Chiricahua Mountains: *24*
Christy, William: *63*
Cleveland Street: 87
Clifton-Morenci: 22, 48, 52, *137*
Cochise: *91*
Cole, A.W.: 108
Colorado River: *27*, *169*
Collins, J.H.: *65*
Colter, Fred T.: 110
Copper Queen Mine: *57*
Congress Mine: 48
Crutchfield, James E.: 110
Crutchfield, Seaborn: 108
Cuniff, Michael: 152
Cunningham, Donnel L.: 110
Curry, George: 144

D

Davis, Arthur Powell: 117, 120
de Coronado, Francisco Vasquez: 14
de Espejo, Antonio: 14
de Oñate, Juan: 14
Dedera, Don: 143
Dorris Opera House: *55*
Douglas: *83*, *106*, 172
Douglas, James: 57
Drachman, Harry Arizona: *94-95*
Dunlap, Three-Finger Jack: 35

E

Earp, Morgan: 35
Earp, Virgil: 35
Earp, Wyatt: 32, 35
Ellinwood, Everett E.: 110

F

Fall, Albert: 144
Fels Naptha soap: 90
Fergusson, Harvey: 144
Flagstaff: 19, *61*, 78, 138, *166-167*
Florence: *166*
Fontana, Bernard: 87
Ford Hotel: 138
Franklin, Alfred: 110, 152
First Arizona Legislature: *150-151*, 152
First Arizona Regiment: *171*

G

Gadsden, James: 40
Gadsonia: 138
Geronimo: *12*, 16, 42, 138
Gila County Courthouse: *55*
Gila monster: *49*
Gila River: *166*
Glendale: *137*, 150
Globe: 22, *39*, 52, 138, 164
Goff, John S.: 110
Goldberg, Hazel: 143
Goldwater, Baron: *62*, 143

Goldwater, Barry: 143, *143*, 172
Goldwater, Morris: 110, 122
Goodwin, John: *16-17*, 40
Grand Canyon: 78, *144*
Green Valley: 172
Greene Cattle Co.: 49

H

Hall, Sharlot: 138
Hamilton, Edward: 87, 100
Harrison, Benjamin: 56
Hart, Pearl: *34*
Hawkins Drug Store: *88*
Hawaii: 52
Havasupai man: *13*
Hayden, Carl: 35, 38, 126, *127*, 165, 173
Heard, Dwight B.: *104*
Heintzelman, Sam: 56
Holliday, Doc: 35
Hooker, Henry: 22
Hopi Indians: 173
Hudson Reservoir and Canal Company: 117
Hughes, Louis C.: *65*
Hunt, George W.P.: 64, 87, 108, *109*, 122, 126, 131, 138, *139*, 142, 143, 144, 145, 152-153, 156-157, *164*, 164-165, *165*, 172
Hunt, Helen Duett Ellison: 145

I

Ingleside Inn: *86-87*
Irish, Fred: 52
Irwin, John: 78

J

Jacome, Carlos C.: 110, 122
Jerome: 22, 52, *59*, 63, *85*, *113*, 152, 172
Johnson, David: 152

K

Kelvin: *46-47*
Kibbey, Joseph H.: 56, 62, 131, *131*
Kino, Father Eusebio: 14
Kitchen, Pete: 22
Kofa Mine: *85*
Kolb, Emery: 115

L

La Guardia, Fiorello: *41*
La Paz: 173
Langdon, John: 110
Leroux, Antoine: 40
Lincoln, Abraham: 40, 130
Longfellow Mine: 22
Loretto School: 135
Lost Dutchman Mine: 173
Lount Ice Plant: *64-65*
Lowell Observatory: 78, *78-79*

Arizona Highways Album   **175**

Index

Luke, Frank Jr.: *152*, 170

M
Maricopa County Courthouse: 55
Melczer, Joseph R.: 143
Mesa: 121, 150
Metcalf: 96
Miami: 52
Milton, Jeff: 32, 35
Moeur, Benjamin, B.: 108, 165
Morenci: *58-59*, 98
Mormons: 86
Mossman, Burt: 35, 36, 38, 78
Mowry, Sylvester: 56
Mrs. Stewart's Liquid Bluing: 90
Murdock, John R.: 144
Murphy, Nathan Oakes: 29, 56, 82, 86, 130
McCarthy, J.F.: 38
McClintock, James H.: 117
McCormick, Richard: *17*, 40
McDonald, W.C.: 144
McKee Cash Store: *88-89*
McKinley, William: 48, *51*, 56, 82

N
Nelson, Knute: 86
New Mexico: 40, 82, 86, 100, 108, 130, 131, 144

O
O. K. Corral: 35
Old Oraibi: *11*
Oldfield, Barney: *167*
Orient Saloon: *20-21*
Orme, John P.: 110
Osborn, Sidney P.: 108, 126, 152
Ostriches: *146*

P
Parkview Hotel: *134-135*
Patagonia: *68*
Pattie, James Ohio: 40
Penuimburg, Euretta: *31*
Peters Grocery: *155*
Philippines: 52, 82
Phoenix: 22, *26*, 40, 42, 52, *54*, *69*, 78, 102, 116, 127, 131, 133, 150, *155*, 157, *160*, 172
Phoenix Choral Society: 143
Phoenix Country Club: *137*
Phoenix Daily Herald: 43
Phoenix Gun Club: *73*
Phoenix High School: *54*
Phoenix Indians: 73
Phoenix Indian School: 143
Phoenix Woman's Club: *75*
Pima: *60*
Pinal County Courthouse: 55

Pleasant Valley War: 35
Poland: *113*
Poston, Charles: 56
Prescott: 22, 40, *66-67*, 78, 102, 130, *135*, 138, *140-141*, 168
Prescott Elks: *74-75*
Prescott High School: *96-97*
Princess (Princes) Bakery: *154*
Prohibition: 153, 156, *157*
Puerto Rico: 52, 82
Pyle, Howard: 172

Q
Q Ranch: *24-25*

R
Ray: 22
Reliable Auto & Blacksmith Shop: *166-167*
Rhodes, John: 172
Riordan, Mike: 19
Riordan, Tim: 19
Roberts, Charles M.: 110
Roberts, Jim: 32, 35-36
Ronstadt Hardware: *154*
Roosevelt Dam: 96, *117*, *119*, 121, 150
Roosevelt Street: 87
Roosevelt, Theodore: 48, 56, 82, *83*, 87, *116*, 120, *120-121*, 131
Ross Drug Store: *62*
Ross, Garland: 30
Rough Riders: 48
Russellville: *99*

S
Sabino Canyon: *94-95*
Safford: 168
Saguaro cacti: *70-71*
Salome: *113*
Salt River: 116, 117
Salt River Canyon: 168
Salt River Project: 121
Salt River Valley: 22, 43, 78, 96, 116, 172
San Marcos Hotel: 150
San Xavier del Bac: *14-15*, 40
Scottsdale: 150, *160*
Shumate Soda Fountain: 88
Silver King Mine: *26*
Simms, Mit: 110
Sky Harbor International Airport: 90
Sloan, Richard E.: 62, 100, *102*, 108, *111*, 131, 145
Smith, Dean: 165
Smith, Marcus Aurelius: 29, 82, *82*, 126, 130, 131, 172
Socialist Party: 63
Sonnichsen, C.L.: 131
Squaw Peak: 145
St. Johns: *162-163*
St. Mary's Hospital: *68*

Stiles, Billy: 36
Sun City: 172
Superstition Mountains: *59*

T
Taft, William Howard: 62, 87, 100, 102, 108, *124-125*, 126, 131, 138, 144, 145
Tempe: *19*, 43, *60*, 150, *154*
Territorial Insane Asylum: 22, *53*
Territorial Normal School, Flagstaff: 78
Territorial Normal School, Tempe: 52, *97*, 143
Tombstone: 22, *44*, 173
Tonto Basin: 116, 117, 121
Tovrea, Edward A.: 110
Trennert, Robert A.: 29
Trimble, Marshall: 38
Tucson: 22, 40, 43, 52, 78, 82, *107*, 131, 138, 150, *154*, 157
Twentieth Legislative Assembly of 1899: *50-51*

U
United Verde Mine: 22
University of Arizona: 29, *53*, 78, *97*, 138

V
Valley Bank Center: 172
Valley Bank of Phoenix: 63
Villa, Pancho: 152

W
Wade, Benjamin: 16
Wagoner, Jay J.: 157
Walker, Joseph: 40
Weaver, Pauline: 40
Weedin, Thomas: *122*, 126
Weinberger, Jacob: 110
Wells, Edmund W.: 108, 144
Wickenburg: 22, *154*
Williams, Ben: 57
Williams, Bill: 40, *41*
Williams, J.S.: 126
Wilson, Maggie: 93
Wilson, Woodrow: 152
Winsor, Mulford: 110, 138, *139*
Women's Suffrage: 153, 156, *157*
Woodson Brothers: 38

Y
Yarnell Hill: 168
Yavapai County Courthouse: 138
Yoas, Bravo Juan: 35
Yuma: 156, 168, *168-169*, 172

Z
Zarbin, Earl: 121
Zulick, Meyer: 130